Further Praise for
Writing History in the Global Era

"In admirably clear prose, Lynn Hunt reports back on the state of the field, reviewing not only how the discipline of history has evolved, but also what it means to write history now, in the shadow of globalization, climate change, and new psychological understandings of the self. Hunt brings to this task her characteristic (and rare) blend of compelling argument and evenhandedness. This is a book that all students of history will need to read and grapple with."
—Sophia Rosenfeld, University of Virginia

"With characteristic concision and lucidity, Lynn Hunt takes on the methodological dilemmas facing all historians today. How should we think of history in a postnational era? What is gained and lost by 'going global'? What happens to individual actors and agency when history is written on a transnational scale? *Writing History in the Global Era* draws on a wide range of writings from the humanities and the social and biological sciences to propose a thought-provoking snapshot of where historians stand now and where they might be headed. Lively and engaging, this book will help both budding and seasoned historians understand the current state of their discipline."
—Sarah Maza, author of
The Myth of the French Bourgeoisie

"Hunt has published a fine book. In the U.S. and beyond, the pages of *Writing History in the Global Era* will virtuously underpin a thousand, thousand doctorates."
—*Times Higher Education*

"A noted historian offers a lucid overview of her changing field. . . . Hunt offers some startling examples of global interaction.

. . . In this incisive look at the history of history, Hunt asserts that globalization will inspire a new paradigm."

—*Kirkus Reviews*

Praise for Lynn Hunt's previous work
Inventing Human Rights: A History

"A tour de force."

—Gordon S. Wood, *New York Times Book Review*

"Elegant . . . intriguing, if not audacious. . . . Hunt is an astute historian."

—Joanna Bourke, *Harper's*

"Fast-paced, provocative, and ultimately optimistic. Declarations, she writes, are not empty words but transformative; they make us want to become the people they claim we are."

—*The New Yorker*

"A provocative and engaging history of the political impact of human rights."

—Gary J. Bass, *New Republic*

"This is a wonderful story of the emergence and development of the powerful idea of human rights, written by one of the leading historians of our time."

—Amartya Sen

"Rich, elegant, and persuasive."

—*London Review of Books*

"As Americans begin to hold their leaders accountable for the mistakes made in the war against terror, this book ought to serve as a guide to thinking about one of the most serious mistakes of all, the belief that America can win that war by revoking the Declaration that brought the nation into being."

—Alan Wolfe, *Commonweal*

WRITING
HISTORY
IN THE
GLOBAL ERA

WRITING
HISTORY
IN THE
GLOBAL ERA

LYNN HUNT

W. W. NORTON & COMPANY
New York   London

To Margaret Jacob

For information about permission to reproduce selections from this book,
write to Permissions, W. W. Norton & Company, Inc.,
500 Fifth Avenue, New York, NY 10110

For information about special discounts for bulk purchases, please contact
W. W. Norton Special Sales at specialsales@wwnorton.com
or 800-233-4830

Manufacturing by LSC Harrisonburg
Book design by Helene Berinsky
Production manager: Devon Zahn

Library of Congress Cataloging-in-Publication Data

Hunt, Lynn, 1945–
Writing history in the global era / Lynn Hunt. — First edition.
pages cm
Includes bibliographical references and index.
ISBN: 978-0-393-23924-9 (hardcover)
1. Historiography—Philosophy. 2. Globalization. 3. History—Philosophy.
4. Historiography—Social aspects. 5. Historiography—Political aspects.
6. Agent (Philosophy) 7. Intellectual life—Philosophy. I. Title.
D13.H856 2014
907.2—dc23

2014011435

ISBN 978-0-393-35117-0 pbk.

W. W. Norton & Company, Inc.
500 Fifth Avenue, New York, NY 10110
www.wwnorton.com

W. W. Norton & Company Ltd.
15 Carlisle Street, London W1D 3BS

5 6 7 8 9 0

CONTENTS

CONTENTS

ACKNOWLEDGMENTS

More than most books, this one had a serendipitous journey. When I gave a talk on the future of cultural history to a graduate student conference at the University of California, Irvine, some years ago, Hans Medick and Doris Bachmann, noted cultural theorists in Germany, happened to be in the audience. Hans invited me to come to his seminar in Berlin and present a fuller version of the talk, which was then published in the journal *Historische Anthropologie*, with which he had long been associated. When I gave talks on the subject at the University of Pisa and the University of Padua, my Italian hosts, Alberto Banti, Vinzia Fiorino, and Carlotta Sorba, prevailed upon me to write up my thoughts in a longer format for their new series on cultural history at Edizioni ETS. That version, *La storia culturale nell'età globale*, translated by Giovanni Campolo, appeared in 2010. I am immensely grateful to these friends and colleagues for pushing me to think through the issues in more sustained fashion and to Giovanni for his painstaking work.

Even then, I was not entirely satisfied with my rendition of the prospects of cultural history, and so various friends consented to read through the English version and suggest areas for improvement. Suzanne Desan, Sarah Maza, Marcy Norton, Jacques Revel, Sophia Rosenfeld, and Vanessa Schwartz read it and offered invaluable suggestions. They may not be satisfied with all of my responses to their remarks, but I hope they know how much I appreciate their willingness to give up their precious time. Along the way, I decided that the subject should not be cultural history but rather the larger domains of cultural theory and globalization. Margaret Jacob helped get me on track with complaints about my dropping too many names into the text, but no one did more than my editor at W. W. Norton, Amy Cherry, who ruthlessly weeded out vague, pretentious, or just muddled writing. It's not always the most pleasant feeling to find pencil marks all over one's manuscript, but I know that in so far as this is a readable book, a lot of the credit goes to her. Needless to say, neither she nor anyone else should be blamed for any inadequacies that remain.

This book is dedicated to the person who has shared and shaped my life for the last twenty-five years, Margaret Jacob.

WRITING
HISTORY
IN THE
GLOBAL ERA

HISTORY'S CHANGING FORTUNES

This is a short book about a big subject, the writing of history in the global era. I wrote it because I believe that two new developments are reshaping the historical landscape. The social and cultural theories that stimulated much history writing from the 1950s onward have lost their vitality, creating uncertainty about how history will be written in the future. At the same time, talk of globalization has proliferated like kudzu; it coils around any attempt to determine the direction of the future or the meaning of the past. Is globalization the new theory that will reinvigorate history? Or will it choke off all other possible contenders, leaving in place only the inevitability of modernization of the world on the Western model?

Despite the continuing popularity of biographies of famous people and books about major wars, history is in crisis and not just one of university budgets. The nagging question that has proved so hard to answer is, "What is it good for?" Once upon a time the answer seemed clear. In the nineteenth century all male students (only men attended universities) studied ancient Greek and Roman history for the models those histories provided to them as future leaders. The Harvard University catalogue of 1852/53 lists the requirements for admission to the freshman class as knowledge of algebra and geometry, all of Virgil's works and Caesar's commentaries, select orations from Cicero and Latin grammar, select readings from Greek, and the ancient history and ancient geography sections of Joseph E. Worcester's *Elements of History* and *Elements of Geography*, as well as an ability to write Latin and Greek. Once admitted, students would take courses on chemistry, physics, and botany as well as a term each of medieval and modern history, but the classics of Greek and Latin literature remained a core of the curriculum right into senior year.[1]

In the late nineteenth and early twentieth centuries, history took on a new role, that of teacher to the nation. History reinforced and in many cases created national identity. Students, especially in the primary and secondary schools, learned that they belonged to a nation because they shared a common past, even if they or their parents were immigrants. In a report published in 1911 for the American Historical Association on teaching in the schools, the authors insisted that American history could not be sacrificed even if schools taught only (!) three years of history as opposed to four: "The simple truth is that these subjects [American history and government] should be given the time they need in the school curriculum, and if shearing and clipping must be done somewhere let the operation be applied to subjects that are not the best and most immediate subjects for preparing boys and girls for citizenship."[2] As history faculties in the universities expanded, national history (American history in the United States, French history in France, etc.) became increasingly dominant, eventually eclipsing Greek and Roman history.

The history of nations got its urgency and sense of purpose from the rise of mass politics and culture. The idea that everyone should get some basic education took root in the United States and Western Europe only toward the end of the nineteenth century. Half the American boys and girls between ages five and nineteen were enrolled in school in 1900, the proportion rising to 70 percent in 1940 and 90 percent in 1970.[3] Greek and Roman orations might serve to train the political elite, but of what use were they to the sons and daughters of coal miners or impoverished immigrants attending school for the first time? The incorporation of the masses into the nation required a different approach. The story of the nation's rise provided the common threads to bind together disparate peoples, whether of different ethnic groups, different classes, or different regions.

History consequently grew as a discipline in a symbiotic relationship with nationalism in the nineteenth and twentieth centuries. History provided new countries with a heritage that had been previously suppressed or ignored, and it shored up identity even in the oldest nation-states, such as England and France. The focus on one's own nation is especially evident in the history taught at the lower educational levels. With the rise of universal education and representative government, history was (and is now) taught to students in primary and secondary schools with the chief aim of making them feel kinship with the other citizens of their nation. To take just one recent example from the United States, on March 19, 2009,

Senator Lamar Alexander introduced Bill 659 to the United States Senate "to improve the teaching and learning of American history and civics." It aimed to provide $150,000,000 for fiscal year 2010 to strengthen "programs to teach traditional American history" in elementary and secondary schools. The stated purpose of the bill was to overcome students' lack of knowledge of U.S. history, which was seen as detrimental to their future as citizens: "The strength of American democracy and our standing in the world depend on ensuring that our children have a strong understanding of our Nation's past."[4]

The use of history for the purposes of national unification is even more striking in states that have only recently gained their independence. A blueprint for educational reform in Ukraine, drawn up by the Ministry for Education shortly after Ukraine became independent in 1991, called for "a national form of education, which is founded on the indivisibility of education from the national soil, the organic unity of national history and traditions, [and] the preservation and enrichment of the culture of the Ukrainian people." Since 2001 the history faculty at Taras Shevchenko National University in Kiev has focused its courses almost entirely on state development in Ukraine, with such offerings as "Ukrainians in the World: History, Culture, Life"; "Development of the Primitive and Ancient Society in Ukraine"; and "Problems of the Formation of the Multi-party System in Ukraine (1980s–90s)."[5]

National history is still the bread and butter of history teaching everywhere. In the United States, 39 percent of history faculty in the colleges and universities teach U.S. history. The next biggest category, European history, accounts for just over one-fourth of the faculty. The figures for national history in France, the United Kingdom, and Germany are even higher, in the German case reaching to nearly half. The obsession with one's own nation is not limited to Western Europe and the United States, as the case of Ukraine shows. At the University of Delhi, all thirteen members of the history faculty who are listed as full professors specialize in Indian history. The history faculty at Peking University is less oriented toward national history than its Indian counterpart, but still over half of its faculty specializes in Chinese history. In the School of History at Australian National University, two-thirds of the faculty work on Australian history.[6]

While maintaining its preponderance right up to the present, national history has changed, often in dramatic and controversial fashion. Already in the 1950s, the national narratives came under fire, perhaps especially in the United States but also in Europe. Political history, in particular the study of the actions of high-ranking governement leaders or elite politicians, no longer satisfied an increasingly diverse and educated public. Social history—the study of groups outside elite circles—rose to the forefront because it drew attention to the kinds of people who were now enrolling in colleges and universities. In 1967 one-third of American males and one-fifth of American females aged eighteen to twenty-four were enrolled in colleges or universities. In 1988 the percentage of women enrolled (30.4 percent of those aged eighteen to twenty-four) overtook that of men (30.2 percent), and the disparity increased thereafter. And while only 13 percent of African Americans aged eighteen to twenty-four enrolled in colleges or universities in 1967 (compared to 27 percent of whites), the disparity narrowed in the 1970s, increased briefly in the late 1980s and 1990s as white enrollment spurted, and then narrowed again in the 2000s. In 2010 the figures were 38 percent for men aged eighteen to twenty-four, 44 percent for women, 38 percent for whites, and 32 percent for African Americans.[7] Democratization of national history went hand in hand with democratization of the university. The experiences of workers, slaves, indigenous peoples, women, and minorities could no longer be ignored.

The new social history resonated in the United States because of its slave and immigrant past and rapidly expanding universities, but it had its origins in Western Europe and enjoyed a global reach, in part because history as it was practiced in Western Europe influenced the writing of history globally. Albert Soboul's *The Parisian Sans-Culottes in the Year II* (1958) and E. P. Thompson's *The Making of the English Working Class* (1963) provide prime examples. Soboul and Thompson aimed to change their own national narratives by highlighting the story of lower-class militancy, yet their pioneering studies ended up inspiring historians in other nations too. No one who studied the French Revolution—or any revolutionary movement for that matter—could ignore Soboul's findings about the significance of lower-class activists (*sans-culottes* were those who did not wear upper-class knee breeches). Thompson's authority was, if anything, even greater. One Indian historian remarked in 1997 that "Thompson's writings were characterized by their Englishness," but "the influence of his work was global" and especially so in India.[8]

In the United States, the rise of social history helped anchor contemporary movements for labor organizing, feminism, and minority rights of all kinds, thus giving history yet another political purpose: cementing the identities of the excluded around a newly discovered past of prejudice and discrimination. Success brought its own problems in tow, however. Even as the new work created demand for a more inclusive national narrative, it ended up generating conflicts over the direction for future work. Was it enough to add the previously excluded to the national narrative, or did the narrative of the nation-state itself require dismantling?[9]

The acknowledgment of so many kinds of past exclusion undermined consensus about the purpose of history. Was history about making a nation or explaining how making a nation depended on overlooking or forgetting those who had been left out? Was the role of the historian to provide a cohesive national narrative, however narrowly or broadly conceived, or to provide a critique of the defects of any such narrative? Was history even about narrative or truth? Was history just another form of myth or ideology used to justify bias and inequality? History's previous failings now seemed to indict the study of history itself.

To explore these issues, scholars and activists turned to new kinds of theories. Theory itself was not new. As history took shape as an academic discipline in the first half of the twentieth century, historians borrowed from the more theoretically inclined social sciences. Soboul's and Thompson's studies, for example, were deeply rooted in Marxism, and they wrote their books in part as contributions to Marxism as theory. They wanted to know which kinds of workers were most likely to organize and become revolutionaries. Others drew their inspiration from sociological theory, whether that of the French sociologist Émile Durkheim, the German social theorist Max Weber, or their followers. Each of them, like Marx but in opposition to him, offered some version of modernization theory, that is, an account of the distinguishing features of modernity, how they emerged, and where they would take Western society in the future.

Even as modernization theories and Marxism inspired groundbreaking research, historians began to question their validity. The studies of Soboul and Thompson are revealing examples. When published in the late 1950s and early 1960s, their books set off firestorms of controversy even within Marxist circles. Each in their own way had drawn attention to the ways of life and yearnings of militants and given those cultural aspects more importance than the traditional Marxist categories of class or relations to economic production. In short, Soboul and Thompson had revealed the limitations of Marxism—its blindness to culture—even while trying to modify it.

Studies influenced by modernization theory suffered a similar fate. The idea of modernity itself came to be seen as excessively tied to Western values and models of development. The simple truth was that scholars invariably identified the modern in modernization theories with the well-known paths of development in Western Europe and the United States. Max Weber, for example, distinguished between "traditional" forms and modern ones and identified the latter with "rationality." Although Weber himself could be critical of the "rational-legal" forms of authority in modern markets and states, it proved hard to ignore the negative connotations of "traditional" or non-modern ways of life. Traditional authority, according to Weber, lacked clearly defined spheres of competence, impersonal rules, rational ordering of superiors and inferiors, regular systems of appointment and promotion, and so on. The traditional was defined by what it lacked in comparison to the modern.[10]

A focus on culture offered a way out of these impasses, and with that new focus came a host of new theories. Where the theories of the 1950s and 1960s had emphasized material causes and sociological explanations, the new cultural theories drew attention to language, symbols, and ritual, and gave priority to interpretation of meaning over causal explanation. It was no longer a question of explaining why certain kinds of workers revolted, for example, but rather of investigating how workers came to think of themselves as different in the first place. The new cultural theories were grouped together under various and often confusing labels: the linguistic turn, poststructuralism, postmodernism, postcolonialism, cultural studies, or just plain "theory." The first chapter of this book aims to explain why these cultural theories arose when they did, what unified them, and why their prominence raised new questions about the purpose of history. The question of purpose is especially vital since the new cultural theories encouraged skepticism about the possibility of establishing truth in history and sometimes led to assertions that history as an academic discipline was inherently Eurocentric and therefore of limited use in the present.

Once the promise and disappointments of this turn to cultural theories have been examined, it will be easier to see why globalization has become such a powerful talking point in recent years. Cultural theories helped blow apart the consensus about the utility of history but failed to offer a compelling alternative to the earlier social theories. Globalization is that kind of compelling alternative. It tells a global story, even though it often still privileges the West, and it offers a return to the "big questions," such as how and why the West rose to global hegemony. Where cultural theories emphasized the local and the micro-historical, talk of globalization inherently underlines the importance of the transnational and macro-historical developments. It also offers a new purpose for history: understanding our place in an increasingly interconnected world. Chapter 2 examines the rise of the globalization paradigm and its consequences for historical study.

Globalization is not the only possible alternative, however, and it is not without its own problems of explanation. While globalization may influence many aspects of life, its impact is uneven and in some cases very limited. Globalization may bring millions of new immigrants into the primary schools of the United States, for example, but just how they are received depends on local cultures, regional economies, and national politics, all of which have to be examined in order to get a more complete picture. The global frame of reference is not always the most relevant one. In chapters 3 and 4, therefore, I return to some of the classic questions of social and cultural theory and offer some new answers to them. The most fundamental of these questions concern the crucial categories of "society" and "self." The meaning of society and self is often taken to be self-evident—if I refer to American society I assume you know what I mean—but when examined more closely, both categories turn out to be ambiguous. By probing the sources of the ambiguity, we can get a better handle on these categories, for they remain essential building blocks for any social or cultural analysis. With renewed attention to society and self, it will be possible to develop new perspectives on history that incorporate some of the critical views that emerged from social and cultural theories in the last decades even while challenging others.

It may seem that the past is by definition over, but the past is always changing because historians and the purposes of history are changing too. When we look for new things in the past—examples of political leadership in ancient times, the story of the rise of the nation, accounts of the persecution and exclusion of certain groups, the spread of globalization—we end up finding unexpected sources and coming to unforeseen conclusions. This variety is not a sign of the fragility or frivolity of history or the inherent biases and prejudices of historians. Seeing cannot take place without a standpoint. The constant evolution of the purpose of history is a sign, rather, of its vitality. Every new age looks for an understanding of its place in time, and without history it would not have one.

ONE

THE RISE AND FALL OF CULTURAL THEORIES

Cultural theories gained traction from the 1970s onward because they offered compelling criticisms of history as it was usually written. There were four major paradigms of historical research in the post–World War II era: Marxism, modernization, the Annales school, and, in the United States especially, identity politics. Each of them came under attack from one or another variety of cultural theory. Some might question whether these four constitute "paradigms" in the sense of Thomas Kuhn, who gave currency to the term in his analysis of the nature of scientific revolutions. Since the publication of his influential work in 1962, scholars have debated the precise meaning of Kuhn's usage and its applicability to other fields. The term caught on because it proved to be useful, and I have no hesitation about employing it, though the reader deserves to see my definition of it. By "paradigm" I mean an overarching account or meta-narrative of historical development that includes 1) a hierarchy of factors that determine meaning, and that hierarchy in turn sets 2) an agenda for research, that is, shapes the choice of problems deemed worthy of study as well as the approaches considered appropriate to use to carry out those studies.[1]

Each of these four major paradigms fits my definition, even though many scholars might complain, with good reason, that there is no one Marxism, no unified modernization approach, no Annales "school," and no single party platform for identity politics. Marxism is the most easily identifiable paradigm because it has an ultimate source in the writings of a single man. In Marx's view, unceasing class struggle eventually leads to the triumph of the workers over their capitalist masters and the establishment through revolution of a communist society. All history is driven by changes in the economic mode of production that shape conflicts between classes. When factories with machines displaced hand weavers, for example, a working class emerged that would organize and contest the control of factory owners. Marxism therefore encouraged study among historians of such specific modes of production as ancient slavery, feudalism, and capitalism, as well as revolutions, labor movements, and the history of the socialist and communist parties. The writings of Soboul and Thompson discussed in the introduction clearly fit into this pattern.

The paradigm of modernization cannot be linked in the same way to the writings of one person, though the inspirations provided by the late-nineteenth-century social theorists Durkheim and Weber are central. Durkheim and Weber are often cited with Marx as the three founding theorists of sociology. Durkheim and Weber sought non-Marxist explanations for the coming of modernity. In place of capitalist production,

Durkheim emphasized the increasing division of labor—the specialization of functions in the workplace. As society became more complex and differentiated, the old shared values broke down, leading to a sense of social alienation or *anomie*. New values like human rights were required. Weber drew attention, as we have seen, to increasing rationalization through the growth, for instance, of state bureaucracies, but he too saw a potentially negative side to this modernization; bureaucratization could become an "iron cage" or "a polar night of icy darkness," hardly an image of liberation. Still, both men considered modernization inevitable.[2]

When the ideas of Durkheim and Weber were incorporated into the modernization paradigm in the 1950s and 1960s, their critical views of modernity were largely left to the side. Sociologists and political scientists, especially in the United States, held up the Western path of modernization as a model for the rest of the world. "Modernity" in this view was a universal category. Although the reputation of modernization theory was severely tested by the defeat of the United States in Vietnam, it is far from moribund. "Modernity" remains a key concept in historical writing, even among historians who wish to have no association with modernization theory. The periodization or division between ancient, medieval, and modern history is still widely accepted; and important elements of modernization theory have reappeared in writings about globalization.[3]

Building upon the insights of Durkheim and Weber, the paradigm of modernization emphasizes the increasing differentiation of knowledge and social functions; the expansion of state powers; and the growing density of communication through urbanization, migration, and new technologies.

In contrast to Marxism, with its emphasis on class struggle between owners and workers, modernization traces conflict to the disparity between modernizing forces and traditional groups who are left behind or resist incorporation into the modern world. The modernization paradigm therefore fosters research into urbanization, migration, technological innovation, social differentiation, and the growth of the state.

Unlike Marxism and modernization theory, which sought to define the distinctiveness of modern industrial society, the Annales school that emerged in the 1930s and 1940s in France focused on preindustrial societies. The school had three main founders, all of them historians: Marc Bloch, Lucien Febvre, and Fernand Braudel. In 1929, Bloch and Febvre, then professors of history at Strasbourg University in eastern France, founded the journal that gave the school its name, *Annales d'histoire économique et sociale*. Published from the very beginning in Paris, where Febvre and Bloch soon lived, in 1946 the journal became *Annales: économies, sociétés, civilisations* and then, after 1994, *Annales: histoire, sciences sociales*. Enthused by Durkheimian sociology, Febvre and Bloch aimed to reorient history away from the traditional study of treaties, battles, and changing regimes toward the study of society, social groups, and collective mentalities. As the various titles of the journal indicate, the Annales school emphasized social and economic history and the relationship between history and the social sciences.[4]

In the late 1930s, Febvre became a mentor to Braudel, who wrote his first book in a German prisoner-of-war camp during World War II. Bloch was tortured and killed by the Gestapo in 1944 because of his role in the French resistance, and Febvre died in 1956. Braudel then took over as chief editor and raised money from American foundations to help set up the Maison des Sciences de l'Homme (House of the Human Sciences). This became the home of the *Annales* and of the École des Hautes Études en Sciences Sociales, the leading school for the study of the social sciences in France. Braudel effectively made the *Annales* the single most influential historical journal of the post-1945 period.[5]

The Annales school of historians believed that environment, climate, and demography shaped human activity in fundamental ways. Since these factors changed slowly over long periods of time, neither revolution nor any other kind of short-term political change concerned them. As Braudel said in the preface to his first book, events were but "surface disturbances, crests of foam that the tides of history carry on their strong backs."[6] What mattered were those tides. As a consequence, the Annales school focused on the centuries from the Middle Ages to the French Revolution, emphasized the slow pace of change, and devoted great energy to developing new techniques for the study of demography in particular. Whereas historians influenced by Marxism studied workers and those using modernization theories focused on migrants or professionals, the Annales school gave pride of place to peasants living in a subsistence economy, making just enough to reproduce their way of life.[7]

The fourth major historical paradigm, identity politics, first took root in the United States in the 1960s and 1970s. Unlike the other paradigms, its main tenets cannot be traced to the inspiration of specific individuals. It arose in response to social movements, such as those for civil rights for African Americans and for women's and gay liberation. Social history, championed by Marxists and Annales-school historians alike, proved fertile ground for the history of excluded and marginalized groups. The history of identities is now spreading across the globe because all countries now face pressing issues about national identity and the role of women, minorities, and immigrants in society and politics.

As its name suggests, identity politics assumes that social identity, whether determined by sex, sexual orientation, race, or ethnicity, is primary, and therefore it inspires research into those social identities, whether of Albanians in Italy, homosexuals in the United States, indigenous women in Peru, or Indian merchants in the diaspora. Although identity politics is not always accompanied by an overarching narrative, the implication of its flowering is that democratization can be achieved only through the inclusion of the previously excluded groups. It also posits that political power depends on control of the national narrative; women, minorities, or immigrant groups can gain their rightful political place only if their contribution to the nation is recognized in histories, museums, and other sites of memory.

The cultural theories that emerged in the 1960s to 1990s undermined these paradigms by challenging the fundamental assumption shared by all of them: that economic and social relations provide the foundation for cultural and political expressions. The culture in cultural theories is not envisioned as a "superstructure" erected on top of the mode or means of economic production, as in Marxism. It is not seen, as modernization theory holds, as the inevitable by-product of changes in social structures, communications, or state bureaucracies. It is not that foam on the sea whose tides are formed by the slow pull of environment and demography, as argued by the Annales school. And it is not the virtually automatic identity determined by a given social position that is assumed by identity politics. Cultural theories overturned those assumptions and insisted instead that culture has its own autonomous logic; language and cultural expressions shape the social world, including the economy, and cannot simply be derived from them.

Where did these cultural theories come from, and what did they argue? The terms used to describe these theories— "cultural studies," "poststructuralism," "postmodernism," "postcolonialism," "linguistic turn," "cultural turn"—have created much confusion. Are they fancy words for the same thing or different things, and do the differences matter?

In my view, these theories are like cousins, closely related through their common affiliation to culture and language. Cultural studies emerged first in Great Britain in the 1950s as Marxists sought to bring Marxism into closer conversation with studies of popular culture and the French theory of structuralism, an anthropological and linguistic approach that drew attention to the influence of underlying cultural structures. When French philosophers began to criticize structuralism, their approach was first termed "poststructuralism," and then it blended into a more general postmodernism. Postmodernism argued that the modern emphasis on reason, truth, science, the autonomous self, and the distinctiveness of humans was merely a product of language; all these categories were unstable, according to postmodernists, and defined only in the course of the exercise of power.

Postcolonialism (sometimes called postcolonial theory or postcolonial studies) applies postmodernism to the situation of formerly colonized peoples; postcolonial theorists examine, for example, how Western hegemony still shapes the categories of thought in supposedly independent countries such as India. "Linguistic turn" was used as a term to lump these developments together under one rubric that emphasized the centrality of language. Since "linguistic turn" seemed to imply a connection to linguistics that did not always pertain, "cultural turn" came to be used as an alternative, especially in the United States. The cultural turn was preferred by those who wanted to maintain the general emphasis on culture without endorsing the philosophical positions of postmodernism. The terms "linguistic turn" and "cultural turn" will be left to the side here, as they are only general descriptions.[8]

Cultural studies are not the same thing as studies of culture. To study culture requires no particular theory, but "cultural studies," as they emerged in Britain, very definitely did. Most histories of cultural studies trace their quickening to the influence of the Jamaican-born British Marxist sociologist and cultural theorist Stuart Hall. A student of youth subcultures, Hall crossbred the increasingly influential cultural Marxism, exemplified by E. P. Thompson, with the French structuralism of the anthropologist Claude Lévi-Strauss, which burst onto the intellectual scene in the 1960s and soon enjoyed international prestige.[9]

After beginning as an attempt to open up Marxism, cultural studies ended up displacing Marxism from the center of British intellectual and political life. Hall argued that traditional Marxism downplayed the importance of ideology and culture with its emphasis on the economics of production. Yet as his brand of cultural studies evolved in dialogue with

French structuralism, ideology and especially culture grabbed center stage.

Lévi-Strauss sought to identify common structures that lay beneath the many different kinship systems around the world. He found them in the rules regulating the exchange of women between kin groups. These rules were not determined by economic conditions but resembled more the conventions of speech. Indeed, according to Lévi-Strauss, "the kinship system is a language." Although he later corrected himself to say that kinship is only *like* a language, the analogy was crucial to him. Emulating those studying phonology (language as a system of sounds), Lévi-Strauss aimed to get at the unconscious structures that systematically organized social relationships.[10]

Both phonology and kinship are based on rules of differentiation rather than on inherent meanings. "Snow" only means snow in English because of its relationship to other sounds and concepts and not because the sound "snow" has any inherent relationship to crystalline water ice. Similarly, possible spouses and prohibited spouses gain their meaning only from the rules of kinship; no one is inherently one or the other. Each society makes its own determination. The rules of language and kinship are produced and reproduced in cultures: they govern the thinking and acting of individuals but are not consciously present in the minds of individuals. Lévi-Strauss showed, in short, that culture has its own rules, its own autonomy, and its own power. As Stuart Hall put it, Lévi-Strauss took what Marxism had labeled "superstructure" and gave it "a specificity and effectivity, a constitutive primacy." One might even say that Lévi-Strauss turned Marxism on its head.[11]

Even as structuralism seemed to carry everything before

it, the French philosopher Jacques Derrida began attacking its assumptions, making him the first poststructuralist. Derrida argued that Lévi-Strauss had set up an untenable dichotomy between nature and culture and had overstated the stability of language and meaning, the coherence of reason, as well as the need for a new humanism. Structures were not as structuring as the term implied; a certain "free play" always escaped from their shaping power. Derrida insisted that "language bears within itself the necessity of its own critique," a critique that would show the indeterminacy that lurks within all dichotomies and supposed binary structures. The philosopher described his own position as one that "tries to pass beyond man and humanism," that is, one that tries to get away from the idea that reason, humanity, or the self can serve as a standard of truth.[12]

"Poststructuralism" lost its salience as a term when structuralism stopped being the main target of attack. "Postmodernism" then became the term of choice because it captured the enormity of the stakes at issue, which were nothing less than the philosophical assumptions inherited from the eighteenth-century Enlightenment that shaped modernity thereafter. Although none of the other postmodernist thinkers devoted as much attention to Lévi-Strauss or wrote in Derrida's distinctively elliptical style, they shared Derrida's focus on "anti-humanism," that is, the endeavor to show how the concept of the human (and reason and freedom) is itself a product of language, not something standing outside of it. In this way, postmodernism made language even more important than it had been for Lévi-Strauss. The thinkers associated with this movement—Derrida, Jacques Lacan, Michel Foucault, and Roland Barthes, among others—sometimes fiercely resented being lumped together as postmodernists. Although the positions of these thinkers were far from identical, the term "postmodernism" has had staying power, as the number of introductory and overview books on the subject attests.

Of the postmodernists, Michel Foucault had by far the greatest influence on cultural studies and on historians in particular. A psychologist and philosopher by training, Foucault set all of his writings in specific historical contexts and paid special attention to the period 1600–1850. In a series of works on the history of madness, the birth of the medical clinic, the emergence of prisons, and the regulation of sexuality (among others), he challenged the standard narrative of the Enlightenment rise of humanitarianism. In the standard narrative, the Enlightenment insistence on reform based on reason brought liberation from the ignorance and brutality of past practices and freed the individual from repressive forces. The modern ways of treating madness, practicing medicine, meting out punishment, and defining sexuality, Foucault countered, actually disciplined people in new and even more insidiously psychological fashion; through observation and examination by others (wardens, teachers, doctors, therapists, priests, social workers) and an insistence on self-monitoring, the modern regimes in effect created the individual in order to control him or her more thoroughly. Rather than reforming society, the new practices reformed—that is, normalized—the individual. The result was conformity, not liberation.[13]

Foucault thus offered a powerful negative perspective on modernity, reason, and individualism. The individual, in his view, was the product of a discourse that emerged between

1600 and 1850 and was therefore contingent, not eternal or universal. It could disappear as readily as it had appeared. In *The Order of Things* (1966) he concluded, "As the archaeology of our thought easily shows, man is an invention of recent date. And one perhaps nearing its end." No person, institution, or social group intentionally created or manipulated this discourse or "discursive formation," the term that Foucault discussed at length in *The Archaeology of Knowledge* (1969). The discursive formation determines what can be said and not said. It shapes the "regime of truth," which is therefore itself contingent, a product of discourse, and at the same time also productive of knowledge. The regime of truth produces knowledge, rather than knowledge producing truth. Truth is not objective, outside power, not a product of a mind liberating itself from prejudice or superstition, as in the Enlightenment narrative. In words that echo Lévi-Strauss's emphasis on structure and system but concern truth rather than kinship, Foucault insisted, " 'Truth' is to be understood as a system of ordered procedures for the production, regulation, distribution, circulation, and operation of statements." There is no truth in the usual sense for Foucault; there is only a politics of truth (in contrast, Lévi-Strauss felt he had penetrated to an absolute and eternal truth about kinship).[14]

Foucault's assault on truth, reason, and humanitarianism stimulated research on a host of fascinating historical issues. Was homosexuality an identity created only in the nineteenth century? Why did prisons put such a premium on surveillance as a part of rehabilitation? How did judicial torture relate to the Old Regime version of sovereignty? Why did the medicalization of madness occur when it did, and what purposes did it serve? In short, by challenging the assumption that the meanings of homosexuality, prisons, torture, and mental illness are self-evident, Foucault compelled historians to reconsider their categories and tools of analysis as well as their conclusions.

Beyond the critique of specific approaches and framing of questions, postmodernism inevitably returned to the basic philosophical questions. If, as postmodernism argues, language shapes all knowledge and experience and there is no standpoint outside language, then truth seems impossible to attain. There is only the truth determined by a particular discursive formation. The postmodernists thus ended up posing the classic problems of philosophical relativism. These philosophical issues provoked wide-ranging debates, not just among historians but also among intellectuals in a variety of fields.

Since they focused on philosophical questions of language and truth, postmodernists such as Derrida and Foucault did not bother much with the four paradigms of historical research. But historians influenced by cultural studies and postmodernism did come up against them and offered convincing criticisms. Historians interested in culture and language insisted that social or economic factors could no longer be assumed to determine in lockstep fashion the content of consciousness, culture, or language. Social and economic categories—homosexuals or money, for example—only came into being through their linguistic and cultural representations. The causal chain itself could no longer be clearly delineated; linguistic and cultural representations did not so much precede social categories or take priority over them as much as they were intertwined with them. Clifford Geertz famously championed this blurring of the causal lines in anthropology by arguing for the importance of "thick description": "Culture is not a power, something to which social events, behaviors, institutions, or processes can be causally attributed; it is a context, something within which they can be intelligibly—that is, thickly—described."[15]

Criticism of the four paradigms came at an opportune moment in the 1960s, 1970s, and 1980s, for they had been weakened already by the force of events. Modernization theories fell on hard times first when the nation-building policies it inspired in the Third World, especially in Vietnam, failed. Marxism steadily lost its appeal after the Soviets crushed the Hungarian uprising of 1956, and then suffered a near fatal blow when the communist regimes collapsed in Eastern Europe and the Soviet Union at the end of the 1980s. The Annales school's emphasis on the slowly changing contours of peasant societies was bound to give way to approaches that gave priority to the kinds of rapid changes in social and cultural life experienced in the West in the post–World War II period. Identity politics, too, faced inevitable transformation as class and sex differences within minorities and increasing rates of mixed marriage altered the meaning of identity.

The four paradigms produced their own gravediggers. Cultural theories appealed in the first instance to scholars who had originally been trained in one of the four paradigms. Joan Scott, one of the leading proponents of postmodernist positions among historians, began her career as a Marxist-inspired labor historian. Geertz, the anthropologist who did the most to bring culture and language to the forefront in the United States, studied under Talcott Parsons, who made the modernization theories of Durkheim and Weber central to American sociology. The Annales-school historians Roger Chartier and Jacques Revel, who pioneered the turn toward culture in France, wrote their first studies using the quantitative techniques of the school. The crossover from identity politics is less apparent, however. The path toward queer studies, for example, was not cleared by historians of homosexuality but rather by scholars outside of history, such as the anthropologist Gayle Rubin and the philosopher Judith Butler. They brought structuralist and postmodernist approaches to bear on the question of sexuality.[16]

The tremors set off by the overturning of the hierarchy of factors shaping meaning could be felt in every field of history. The French Revolution, to take one example, could no longer be viewed as the victory of capitalism over feudalism, as it had long been described in Marxist historiography. Instead, it became a revolution in political culture, in which language, ritual, and symbols played a transformative role. Culture shaped class and politics rather than the other way around. François Furet set the mold for this kind of interpretation when he argued that the French Revolution "inaugurated a world in which the representations of power are the center of the action, and in which the semiotic circuit is the absolute master of politics." When the monarchy collapsed, the vacuum of power was filled by struggles to represent or speak for the people. Speech substituted for power and reshaped social relations rather than simply expressing them. The same kind of approach soon appeared in the study of virtually every modern revolution.[17]

As modernization theory lost its credibility, historians of the non-West turned toward "area studies," the studies of regions such as Africa, South America, and East Asia. Area studies did not demand a specific theoretical commitment and could foster an interest in the particularities of different cultures. In the face of continuing resistance to modernity in many places, such as Iran after the fall of the shah, some former followers of modernization theory came to see the focus on rationality as problematic and urged research instead into community values. Postmodernism only reinforced this questioning of modernity and its rationality.[18]

The editors of *Annales* captured the sense of sea change in a 1988 editorial: "The dominant paradigms, which used to be sought in various kinds of Marxism or structuralism or in the confident use of quantification, have lost their organizing capacity at a time when ideologies have fallen into disrepute." They had no specific recommendations to make in response, however, other than to draw attention to the usefulness of micro-history, the study of a person or a village, as opposed to the Annales school's customary focus on a region of France or a broader geographic region such as the Mediterranean. The editors sensed the upheavals taking place in the study of history, but they were not certain what they would produce.[19]

Identity politics went through particularly wrenching transformations because the history of identity groups had been central to their political demands. Consider, for example, the history of women. Historians of women dug up significant new evidence about the role of women as rulers, writers, suffragettes, industrial laborers, and wives and mothers in order to show that women had played important roles in the past. Yet scholars animated by cultural theories now argued for a history of gender, not women. What mattered, in the view of gender historians, was not the social category women but rather the cultural and discursive means by which the category itself was constructed. The difference was far from semantic. Gender relations—the cultural system of differentiating between women and men—could not be grasped by studying what women did or even thought. Attention had to be paid to the whole system of sex-based interactions, in particular to what men said and did; in short, those relationships had to be theorized in cultural terms. Women themselves were in danger of receding once again into the background.[20]

Similarly, the study of African Americans, Asian Americans, and Latinos was challenged by race studies; the history of homosexuality, by queer studies; and the history of indigenous peoples, by postcolonial studies. In each case, histories that presumed the existence of social categories were contested by cultural critiques that focused on the construction and therefore deconstruction of those categories. Examination of the experience of oppression of African Americans, homosexuals, and indigenous peoples began to seem less crucial than the analysis of the language and categories of race and sexuality, and those in power, not the oppressed people, defined the categories.

Studies of an astonishing variety of times and places showed that race, gender, and class could not be viewed as stable categories determined by biology, demography, or economics. Each of them was shaped by unstable systems of interrelationship created by shifting cultural values. To be black, for example, turned out not to be a question of skin color, much less an underlying genetic variation (there is more genetic variation within than between races), but rather a question of the defining power of "whiteness." White and black were cultural representations. In the nineteenth-century United States, "whiteness" depended on one's degree of freedom, level of civilization, and adherence to Christianity, as well as skin color. Christians were considered whiter than non-Christians, Protestants whiter than Catholics, and immigrants from northern Europe whiter than those from southern Europe. Between the 1840s and 1880s, Irish immigrants, for instance, were portrayed as apelike, dependent, and more like Chinese or blacks than whites. They only gradually came to be represented and perceived as white.[21]

Since the previous hierarchy of factors determining meaning had crumpled, it followed that the agenda for research would change as well. Examination of cultural representations took priority over the analysis of social and economic conditions. The progression of research undertaken in response to E. P. Thompson's book *The Making of the English Working Class* can serve as a handy example. In the book Thompson had insisted that "the class experience is largely determined by the productive relations into which men are born—or enter involuntarily," a standard Marxist assertion. His hundreds of pages on that experience nonetheless helped stimulate cultural studies because in those pages he paid much more attention to workers' language, rituals, and habits of mind than he did to socioeconomic structures.[22]

In the next generation, influenced by postmodernism as Thompson was not, historians focused ever more intently on workers' language, arguing that Thompson had failed to grasp the need for a proper linguistic analysis. For all his attention to culture, they maintained, Thompson had incorrectly assumed that workers' language simply reflected their experiences rather than shaping those experiences in the first place. Feminist historians complained, in addition, that Thompson had missed the ways in which male working-class language and culture effectively pushed women to the side, relegating them to a sphere of domesticity even though women were actively participating in working-class movements. Thompson himself vociferously rejected the view that historians needed cultural theories, in particular those imported from France.[23]

Despite the resistance of some leading historians such as Thompson, cultural theories steadily extended their influence on the research and writing of history. Cultural history, the field most attentive to cultural theories, eventually achieved a kind of dominance in the United States. For fifteen years after the mid-1990s, cultural history was the single most popular subject designation among members of the American Historical Association, followed closely by religion and women's history. Political and even social history lagged far behind; indeed between 1992 and 2004 the number of historians identifying with the category social history—aligned variously with Marxism, the Annales school, and identity politics—shrank by two-thirds.[24]

Cultural history and cultural studies established their beachheads in the Anglophone world first. Only recently have efforts begun to examine the international dimensions of the trend. The International Society for Cultural History was founded only in 2008, and four years later it began publishing its flagship journal, *Cultural History*. Recent overviews of cultural history have appeared in at least eight languages, all of them European. Cultural studies, more general than cultural history because they combine British Marxism with postmodernism in investigating popular culture and media as well as history, have developed audiences in India, China, and some African countries, but their reception remains uneven.[25]

Despite the growing influence of cultural theories, their relationship with non-Western countries remains paradoxical: the approaches of postmodernism have been used to criticize Eurocentrism, but at the same time, most of the elements of those critiques have been derived from Western sources. Since cultural theories trace their origins primarily to Britain (cultural studies), France (postmodernism), and the United States (cultural history), they might even be viewed as a by-product of Western imperialism. Still, postmodernist positions about the inevitable contingency of truth have resonated powerfully with those who seek to contest Western intellectual hegemony and in effect "provincialize" Europe, as the Indian historian Dipesh Chakrabarty has advocated.

Chakrabarty drew attention to the fact that Third World historians must read the leading works in European history, while European historians can ignore work from and about elsewhere because European historians provide a supposedly universal model for history scholarship. "Whether it is an Edward Thompson, a Le Roy Ladurie, a Georges Duby, a Carlo Ginzburg, a Lawrence Stone, a Robert Darnton or a Natalie Davis . . . the 'greats' and the models of the historian's enterprise are always at least culturally European." Chakrabarty wants to change that situation, but as he himself recognizes, most of his tools of critique come from an engagement with the European intellectual tradition, especially postmodernism.[26]

The example of Chakrabarty shows, nonetheless, that cultural theories, however much indebted to European sources, can be turned against Eurocentrism. The use of postmodernism to critique Eurocentrism has been labeled "postcolonialism," so called because it entails a challenge to colonial ways of knowing, in particular, the supposed superiority of Western ways of knowing. The patron saint of postcolonialism is Edward Saïd, the late Palestinian American professor of English and comparative literature whose book *Orientalism* (1978) turned postmodernism back on the West. Saïd explicitly relied on Foucault's insight that power shapes truth. In Saïd's view, the West created "the Orient" in the image of its own prejudices; "European culture gained in strength and identity by setting itself off against the Orient." The Orient was weak because it was effeminate; the West, strong because it was virile. The Orient was despotic; the West, parliamentary. The Orient was mysterious, secretive, and sensual; the West, straightforward, open to the public, and gentlemanly. Western scholars, diplomats, and administrators developed this Orientalism as a tool of their imperial power, and using it, they sought knowledge of Oriental culture to serve their own ends. Thus, as Foucault had insisted, knowledge serves power rather than speaking truth to power or offering any liberation from it.[27]

The postcolonial inflection of cultural theories has had a wide influence. In fact, when Chakrabarty originally published his indictment of the authority of European history in 1992, the tide was beginning to turn. Western historians now read histories of the non-West and are expecting to find material and approaches that will influence their work (Chakrabarty's writings being a prime example). They must do so if only because they have become much more aware of the embeddedness of their supposedly European subjects in a global context. Just as France can no longer be conceived as extending only to the boundaries of the hexagon (as the mainland is called, based on its shape) since its former colonies have been part of its history for hundreds of years and remain so even after decolonization, so too European history can no longer be conceived as merely about Europe. Europe has been involved in the exchange of goods, ideas, and people with the Middle East, Africa, Asia, and the Americas for centuries. Europe is only Europe, as Saïd taught, in opposition to somewhere else. Identity is the product of a relationship, not an internal essence. Identity is not a sameness after all; it is a difference from something else.[28]

The rise of these various cultural theories inevitably set off alarm bells, and Thompson was not alone in hearing them. The Marxist historian Eric Hobsbawm described his reaction: "As French thinkers increasingly moved into the territory of 'postmodernism' I found them uninteresting, incomprehensible, and in any case of not much use to historians." Yet historians were using postmodernism, and that influence bothered, even infuriated, some scholars. The economic historian Stephen Haber reviewed cultural approaches to Mexican history and objected in particular to "a postmodern ambivalence about the existence of objective facts." The new cultural history, he maintained, relied on a subjective view of knowledge that "is fundamentally flawed." Moreover, the political goals of its practitioners, which in the case of Latin American history are "anticapitalist, prosocialist, and prorevolutionary," inevitably distorted their analysis. In his view, postmodern relativism combined with political bias to fatally undermine the claims of the new cultural history.[29]

The U.S. social historian Paula Fass found cultural history wanting even when it was not directly indebted to postmodernism. "In response to the perceived misplaced certainty of social history," she wrote, "we suffer today from the reverse as cultural history threatens us with fuzziness, inexactness, and analytic solipsism of grand conclusions positioned on erratic data." Cultural historians devote too much attention, she insisted, to marginal people and eccentric documents, and not enough to the normal or mainstream functioning of society. When not defining a culture in terms of an exemplary, but far from typical, individual, cultural historians, she argued, refer instead to vast undifferentiated forces. The critical distinguishing tools of social history need to be revived, she concluded.[30]

By the 1990s even the earlier proponents of cultural theories began to worry about the pitfalls of their success. One of the pioneers of cultural approaches in history, William Sewell, suggested that the very term "culture" risked losing all salience. The "academic culture mania" turned off many anthropologists, he insisted, because the incessant talk of culture exoticized and stereotyped the groups under study. Could cultural historians continue to use such a compromised concept? Sewell thought they could, but only with attention to some serious problems.[31]

Others complained that culture had taken on more explanatory weight than it could bear. The U.S. sociologist Richard Biernacki argued that cultural historians merely inverted the claims of the social historians: "They followed the social historians in building explanations that rest on appeals to a 'real' and irreducible ground of history, though that footing is now cultural and linguistic rather than (or as much as) social and economic." The British geographer Don Mitchell made the claim even more explicit: "There is no such (ontological) thing as culture." Mitchell urged "social theorists" to dispense with it altogether and "begin focusing instead on how the very idea of culture has been developed and deployed as a means of attempting to order, control, and define 'others' in the name of power or profit." Cultural theories, too, were a cultural representation and subject to the same kind of critique those theories had leveled against the four paradigms.[32]

Historians who employ cultural theories thus have been accused variously of ignoring politics and of politicizing their studies, of paying insufficient attention to the agency of human actors and paying too much attention to the agency of all too unique individuals, of attributing too much to words in general and not enough to particular words in specific kinds of social, economic, and political documents. These criticisms, though not without their merits, overlook the rhetorical and political nature of the reference to culture. Cultural theories put the emphasis on culture in order to contest the paradigms that always reduced culture to something else. Proponents of cultural theories or cultural history do not agree on one meaning for culture (or language, or discourse), but frankly they do not worry much about their failure to agree on definitions. They are more interested in rejecting views of culture as an automatic by-product of economic forces or social position. Mitchell's proposal, for example, falls very much into the Marxist view of culture; he sees it as being deployed "in the name of power or profit." Cultural theories refuse that reduction of culture to something else. Power and profit themselves depend on cultural representations.

Yet there is no denying that the prominence of postmodernism in cultural theories and cultural history has been especially contentious. Joan Scott served as a lightning rod of controversy about postmodernism because she played such a prominent role in feminist history and was the most theoretically sophisticated of the pioneers of cultural and gender history. Her book *Gender and the Politics of History* (1988) is one of the most cited works in these fields because it provides both a theoretical overview and specific examples of how postmodernism can inspire historians to view evidence in new ways. It also celebrates the relativism of postmodernism. "A more radical feminist politics (and more radical feminist history)," she insisted, "seems to me to require a more radical epistemology." She turned in particular to Jacques Derrida and Michel Foucault because those authors link knowledge and power and their work "relativizes the status of all knowledge."[33]

Scott's focus on language and discourse troubled many feminists and women's historians. Scott's fellow French historian, Laura Lee Downs, captured the frustration of many with the notion that woman was simply a discursive construction when she titled a critical essay "If 'Woman' is Just an Empty Category, Then Why Am I Afraid to Walk Alone at Night? Identity Politics Meets the Postmodern Subject." In a critique largely aimed at Scott's work, Downs admitted the pertinence of postmodernism's challenge to Western knowledge but lamented that it effectively killed off the individual person as a knowing subject and as a foundation for political action.

Other critics were even harsher. In "Gender as a Postmodern Category of Paralysis," a leading historian of women, Joan Hoff, complained that the postmodernist emphasis on deconstructing the category of woman threatened to sever women's history from its political foundation and mission. Postmodernism, in her view, was bad for feminist history.[34]

Since postcolonialism, too, was closely identified with postmodernism, it proved susceptible to the same kinds of criticisms. Viewing the native or aborigine as simply a product of discourse ends up paralleling the problem with woman as an empty category. The experience of the aborigine no longer matters nearly as much as the discursive formation that establishes aborigine as a meaningful category, and the discursive formation always invariably confers power on the white, male, non-aborigine who defines the terms of discourse. In postcolonialism, the reliance on European theoretical models derived from Foucault, Derrida, and other postmodernists proved especially problematic. White, male, European and Eurocentric academics provided the cultural theories that appeared to diminish the capacity of postcolonial peoples for acting in their own names. Latin America simply became an object of study or an ideological construct like the Orient, as Abril Trigo complained. Latin America ceases to have any existence of its own.[35]

Much ink has been spilt on the subject of postmodernism, and I find little point in rehearsing all the arguments once again, especially since disputes about its influence have largely subsided. After considerable hand-wringing about the need to recapture experience, reestablish the potential for human agency, and find some basis for claims of truth, most historians have simply moved on, incorporating insights from postmodern positions but not feeling obliged to take a stand on its epistemological claims. Derrida and Foucault still appear in introductions to cultural studies, to be sure, but epistemological questions (Is there truth? How do we know it?) have faded into the background. "Theory" no longer excites the same enthusiasm or fury.[36]

What remains is the study of culture, but to what end? The four paradigms of historical research—Marxism, modernization, the Annales school, and identity politics—lost their standing, but cultural theories did not offer a compelling alternative. They were better at tearing down than rebuilding. Culture became a kind of catchall, and in the process culture lost its explanatory power. As the literary theorist Tilottama Rajan complains, "What has given culturalism its current dominance despite its lack of explanatory power is precisely an inclusive vagueness that masks underlying contradictions." What began as a penetrating critique of the dominant paradigms ended up seeming less like a battering ram and more like that proverbial sucking sound of a flushing toilet.[37]

Advancing similar criticisms, William Sewell recently charted his own trajectory from social to cultural history and his growing concerns about the direction of the latter. He was particularly troubled by the retreat from analysis of causes and from "consideration of the dynamics of capitalism." Historians' "new passion for the small, the local, the elementary, the culturally constructed" shared, he thought, "a certain logic" with contemporary capitalism, particularly its drive toward deregulation. In other words, historians' interest in culture kept them from seeing the broader patterns in the development of multinational capitalist finance and enterprise. Although Sewell does not advocate a knee-jerk return to 1970s-style Marxism or modernization theory, like Paula Fass he does urge cultural historians to recapture some of the virtues of social history: the use of quantitative methods; an interest in the experiences of ordinary people and especially the poor and downtrodden; and renewed attention to socioeconomic structures and processes. In the end, he is advocating a kind of updated Marxism.[38]

Must historians choose between a return to the previous paradigms or no paradigm at all? Although history writing is inherently provisional because our sense of the purpose of history is always subject to change, I will argue in the last chapters of this book that we can benefit from a new paradigm. It will not convince everyone or hold forever even among those who are convinced by it. But big histories, overarching stories, or meta-narratives seem to be part of human nature. We want to know where we have come from and we want answers on various scales—of our lives, our nations, our civilizations, our worlds. For all the talk of refusing such accounts—Jean-François Lyotard famously defined the postmodern condition as one of "incredulity toward metanarratives"—they have a way of sneaking back in.[39]

Among the postmodernists, Foucault stood alone in making a postmodern paradigm for history explicit. He not only opposed the modernity narrative of rising humanitarianism and liberation but also offered in its place his own counter-narrative of the rise of the disciplinary society. Modern history, according to Foucault, was not driven by the triumph of capitalism, sexual liberation, democracy, or human rights. Modernity meant rather the emergence of a disciplinary society in which schools, factories, armies, and prisons controlled individuals by shaping their minds and bodies.[40]

Foucault's counter-narrative bore considerable resemblance to Max Weber's account of the "iron cage" of modernity and its bureaucratic rationalism, but Foucault went even further by showing how modern bureaucratic forms themselves produced a sense of individual identity. "These two great 'discoveries' of the eighteenth century—the progress of societies and the geneses of individuals—were perhaps correlative with the new techniques of power," Foucault writes in *Discipline and Punish* (1975), "and more specifically with a new way of managing time" by segmenting it, classifying it, and making total use of every minute. The knowledge and very existence of society and the individual thus were produced by new techniques of power. The individual was simply the efficient nodal point of surveillance and internalization, not the knowing subject who could transform the world through self-conscious agency. Foucault's success at constructing an alternative paradigm made his work immensely fruitful for historians, who could contest it or build upon it. I aim to contest it in the final chapter of this book.[41]

Challenging Foucault's account of modernity requires a more general critique of the assumptions that cultural theories share in the end with the very paradigms they subverted. Even while questioning the reduction of culture and language to economic and social factors, cultural theorists such as Foucault argue that the self, the body, the emotions, and even reason itself are the products of language, discourse, and culture. They are determined by culture and therefore are culturally relative. In the *Encyclopedia of Feminist Theories* (2000), for example, a contributor categorically states that "race, like gender, is largely a product of oppressive social construction . . . in cultures dominated by white men." While proponents of cultural theories insist that language, discourse, and culture have an autonomy and logic of their own, they nevertheless also hold that experience, emotions, and even the sense of individuality and identity are entirely shaped by the meanings that envelop them. Individuals see and respond to the world only through the veil of language or culture. The self and its experience have no autonomy; only culture does.[42]

Cultural theories thus remain "social constructionist" even while shifting attention to different elements in the social realm, that is, to language and culture rather than technology or the mode of production. The realm of the social—whether called society, social relations, identity, culture, or discourse—remains the ground or source of meaning. Cultural theories show that "the social" is more complex than once thought; society does not stand below culture, like a mythological Atlas holding up the sky. Instead the social is the warp and culture the weft, which together weave meaning, experience, and identity. But cultural theories also maintain that there is no meaning, experience, or identity outside of society and culture. This presupposition—that the social is the ground or source of meaning—is a powerful, secular way of understanding the world, and its power has not been exhausted. Yet it is not the only way of understanding the world. In chapter 3, I try to dig more deeply into the operation of the social, especially in relation to the self, and suggest some different ways of thinking about meaning.

By largely (with the exception of Foucault) abdicating the terrain of paradigms, cultural theories left the way open for other paradigms to take the place of Marxism, modernization, the Annales school, and identity politics. Globalization, I will argue in the next chapter, is just such an overarching story, one that includes a new agenda for research. Historians need to contest the terrain it now claims, using the tools held out by cultural theories while remaining mindful of their limitations.

TWO

THE CHALLENGE OF GLOBALIZATION

Historians have only recently discovered globalization. Their neglect of the topic hardly makes them unique, however, as interest in globalization, as shown by increasing use of the word in titles of books, dates only to the 1990s.

It hardly appears at all in titles before the late 1980s, but a sharp increase occurs during the 1990s and continues into the 2000s.[1] The phenomenon of globalization did not start in the 1990s, and there is no agreement about just when it did begin. Since we are all descendants of the colonists from Africa, who replaced other early humans throughout the world 40,000 to 125,000 years ago, globalization has in some sense accompanied human history from the beginning. Some argue, nonetheless, that globalization only truly began with the nineteenth-century revolution in transport and communications, when railroads, steamships, telegraph, and telephones facilitated much faster communication and delivery of goods across great distances. Others see globalization as a

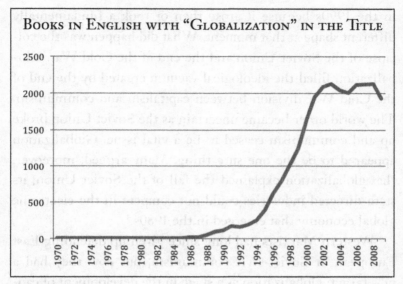

Source: WorldCat

longer-term development, with periods of interruption, that includes the spread of the world religions (Buddhism, Judaism, Christianity, Islam), the European overseas discoveries and conquests, and the resulting European colonization of diverse parts of the globe. The only new element that emerged in the 1990s was the spread of the Internet, but at the time it affected mainly the already developed world. In 2000 only 5 percent of the world's population used the Internet, as compared to 34 percent in 2012. The Internet continues to penetrate and link different regions of the world and is certainly a force in globalization, but the rapid spread that began at the end of the 1990s cannot explain the sudden interest in globalization at the beginning of that decade.[2]

In short, globalization did not suddenly attract attention

in the 1990s because it arose then or took a fundamentally different shape at that moment. What did happen was the collapse of the Soviet Union and the end of the Cold War. Globalization filled the ideological vacuum created by the end of the Cold War division between capitalism and communism. The world order became uncertain as the Soviet Union broke up and communism ceased to be a vital issue. Globalization appeared to be the one sure thing. Many argued, moreover, that globalization explained the fall of the Soviet Union; its state-directed industries could not compete in the electronic global economy that emerged in the 1980s.[3]

Western Marxists had long since given up defending East European or Soviet-style communism, but now they had a new target: globalization as a stage in the development of capitalism. Marxists believed, not surprisingly, that the relentless expansion of capitalism, especially into the former Eastern Bloc and the non-West, was not inevitable, natural, or beneficial to most people. Globalization of capital, in their view, followed from the so-called neoliberal revolution of the 1980s that had been propelled by the policies of Margaret Thatcher in the United Kingdom and Ronald Reagan in the United States. When communism, under the weight of its own contradictions, collapsed, Marxist theorists turned their attention to the conflicts within capitalism, which had not disappeared or lost any of their salience for social analysis. Thus, globalization will be a subject of dispute for some time to come.[4]

Historians were slow to take up globalization as a source of interest. They had their own reasons for ignoring it, chief among them the straitjacket of nation-centered history writing. The fate of a textbook commissioned in 1949 by UNESCO for fourteen-year-old French students is particularly revealing of the pressures of national and nationalist history. UNESCO wanted to encourage "international comprehension" by providing an example of a more capacious national history, one that would show how much every nation, in this case France, owed to other peoples. Officials hoped that this example would encourage other countries to follow suit. The authors, Lucien Febvre, leader of the Annales school, and François Crouzet, a noted French specialist on British economic history, embraced their mission with enthusiasm and produced a model history of the global influences on life in France. Look at the people around you, they suggested. Are they one race? Hardly: one look would convince anyone that the "French" are a mixture of peoples, including Arabs and Africans. Look at the plants in the local park, they continued. The most "French" of trees came from Asia: the plane tree arrived in the mid-sixteenth century, for example, and the chestnut in the early seventeenth. Similarly, many of the most "classic" French foods originated elsewhere: green beans, potatoes, and tomatoes in the New World; citrus in the Far East; and so on. In short, much of the impact of the world on France was already well known sixty years ago. What happened? Febvre and Crouzet's book was published for the first time in 2012, its original publication apparently having been blocked by those who disliked its de-emphasis on the nation and Europe.[5]

Specialization at the university level cemented the bond between professional historians and the national histories they studied, even for those who did not devote themselves to their own national history. An Australian historian might study the Italian Renaissance, for example, but would find it difficult to master, in addition, Francis I's reign in France, much less the Spanish and Portuguese conquest of the Americas, even though these events happened at the same time.

Specialization followed from the drive of history and other social science and humanities fields to emulate science. To be an "expert" meant mastering a field of study, picking a pertinent problem to examine, undertaking research on it, and publishing the findings. A kind of vicious circle ensued: the number of publications increased as universities demanded proof of expertise, and as the volume of publications surged, fields had to be defined ever more narrowly if they were to be mastered. A historian might start off, as I did, specializing in France and then quickly narrow the focus to one region in France, one or two towns, or even one village. For my PhD dissertation and first book, I examined two towns in the region of Champagne, Reims and Troyes, at the end of the Old Regime and the beginning of the French Revolution.[6]

The aim of such studies was always to illuminate the history of France. An analysis of two countries therefore seemed wildly ambitious; if most people were talking about one or two places in one country, how could a historian talk about two countries, with different languages, cultures, and histories? Although historians specializing in pre-1800 time periods might focus on a single Renaissance city-state like Florence or an entire empire such as the Roman, Ottoman, or Holy Roman one, the nation-state has dominated historical research about the modern period. There are few historians of Europe as a whole in the modern period, just historians of France, Great Britain, or Italy, for example; virtually no Asian historians, only specialists on Japan, China, India, Indonesia, or another

Asian country; no historians of the Americas, but rather historians of Canada, the United States, Mexico, or Peru. Historians of Africa sometimes work on more than one former colony but usually only other colonies of the same imperial power.

Yet even nation-centered history writing has begun to stretch under the impact of changes in national identities. In the United States, once workers, women, and African Americans gained admission to the national narrative, new immigrant groups would not be far behind. Since students in the United States now come from all over the world, learning about the world is an important supplemental way of creating national coherence. World history of some kind had been taught in American high schools since their first establishment in the early nineteenth century. Until the 1980s, however, world history generally meant the history of Western civilization. Popular textbooks of the late nineteenth century either failed to say anything about India or China, for example, or mentioned them only in passing while concentrating on ancient Greece and Rome and the history of Europe. The establishment of the World History Association in 1982 marked the moment when world history began to move away from a Eurocentric focus to a more polycentric one. In its teaching guide for the Advanced Placement examination in world history that is administered to high school students planning to attend a college or university, the College Board explicitly cites the growing number of U.S. students from non-European backgrounds and their desire for "history teaching that touches on their own cultural origins as well as on the long-privileged European past."[7]

In contrast to the United States, European nations have to confront not only the challenges of incorporating new immigrants into the national narrative but also those of constructing a European identity as something intermediary between the nation-state and the world. If the European Union is to succeed in the long run, it must be able to call upon a European identity that will support European institutions. A common currency and common border policies are not enough, as the economic crisis of the last few years has revealed. In the late 1990s, Recommendation 1283 of the Parliamentary Assembly of the Council of Europe called upon schools in the European Union to include in their syllabuses "the history of the whole of Europe, that of the main political and economic events, and the philosophical and cultural movements that have formed the European identity."[8]

Still, world history is on the rise in Europe too. The areas announced for the *agrégation* (the examination required to gain access to teaching posts at the secondary level in France) in history for 2013 were the Greek diasporas in the Mediterranean basin and the Indus valley from 800 to 300 BC; war and society from 1270 to 1480 in Scotland, England, Ireland, Wales, France, and the western regions of the Holy Roman Empire; international circulation in Europe from 1680 to 1780; and colonial societies in Africa, the Caribbean, and Asia in the 1850s to 1950s. Even if these topics still give priority to Europe, they represent a considerable broadening out from a narrow national base.[9]

It remains to be seen whether these larger webs of identity (European or global) can soften the edges of national pride and its association with historical scholarship. The case of Ukraine, discussed in the introduction, shows that independence can lead to a turning inward and a new defensiveness about national identity. After the breakup of the former Yugoslavia, both the United Nations and the European Association of History Educators decided to devote international seminars to teaching Bosnian, Croatian, and Serbian histories in ways that would not further inflame hostilities between ethnic groups. History has not lost its mobilizing power. A more globally oriented history might well serve to encourage a sense of international citizenship, of belonging to the world and not just to one's own nationality, but this outcome is as yet far more of a promise than a reality.[10]

Although the reasons for historians' increasing interest in global history are still up for discussion, a major shift is nonetheless occurring: interest in transnational, if not global, history is rapidly increasing. Open any recent issue of the *American Historical Review* and you will find evidence of this change. Long a bastion of scholarly focus on the history of the United States and Western Europe, the *American Historical Review* now regularly publishes pieces in transnational, interregional, and global history. Historians of nation-states, even historians of their own nation-state, are increasingly seeking to put their histories in global context.

Historians of the early United States, for example, always drew attention to the links between American and British history, but now they also link the United States to the Caribbean islands with their slave economies and to the role of the French, Spanish, and Dutch, who also colonized parts of the North American mainland. Similarly, historians of eighteenth-century and revolutionary France now recognize the influence of slavery, not just on the Caribbean islands and the African trading posts where slaves were bought and transported by French merchants, but also on mainland France itself. Since French territories stretch across the world from Martinique in the Caribbean and Saint-Pierre in Canada to New Caledonia in the Pacific, it seems only right to stop limiting French history to its European implantation. Moreover, as Febvre and Crouzet argued sixty years ago, even European France can no longer be viewed as self-evidently French. French cafés, for example, were first set up in seventeenth-century Paris by Armenian merchants, and many of the French did not speak French until late in the nineteenth century. A global history was always lurking behind the veneer that nationalism painted on the past.[11]

Is this increasing attention to the global context of history just an effect of globalization, or might it be one of its causes? Much depends on the definition of globalization and how it functions as an explanation. Is globalization a new paradigm for historical explanation that replaces those criticized by cultural theories? Or is it a Trojan horse that threatens to bring back old paradigms rather than truly offering a new one? Do we risk losing all that we gained from the challenge to the old paradigms in the first place, or can cultural theories offer a critical perspective that helps reshape the globalization debates themselves?

To answer these questions, we first need a definition. Globalization is the process by which the world becomes more interconnected and more interdependent. The emphasis on interdependence is critical because it means that simple contact is not sufficient. Globalization did not occur the moment when Christopher Columbus set foot on an island in the Bahamas in 1492. Globalization occurred only when Europeans developed a taste or use for plants that grew in the Americas (tomatoes, potatoes, corn, chocolate, tobacco) or could be grown there (sugar and cotton with the development of plantation slavery). In other words, globalization increased when Europe and the Americas became dependent on each other, even if their interdependence was far from mutual or equally beneficial. Globalization is not limited to the exchange of goods or foodstuffs. It can be defined in economic, technological, social, political, cultural, or even biological terms.[12]

Although globalization is best viewed as a long-term process running in fits and starts throughout all of human history, most commentators on globalization have focused on the last twenty to thirty years. From this short-term perspective, economic globalization is the worldwide interpenetration of financial institutions, trade networks, and manufacturing circuits (sometimes called multinational or transnational capitalism). Technological globalization compresses time and space through widely accessible air travel, containerized shipping, the spread of computers and with them access to the Internet, and even more recently, global positioning satellites and wireless communication. Social globalization derives from increasing migration from country to country and from countryside to city, especially to the great global megalopolises such as Shanghai, Mexico City, London, and New York City. Political globalization includes attempts to establish world hegemony through arms (the United States) or armed resistance (terrorism), the growing influence of larger political units (European Union, World Trade Organization, United Nations), and global terms of political discussion such as human rights. Cultural globalization is the development of global forms of identity and activities of everyday life: hybrid or diasporic identities grow more important; anime, video games, coffee, Coca-Cola, and airport lounges can be found worldwide; and religious movements (Islam and evangelical Protestantism, for example) increasingly depend on internationalization for their identities. Biological forms of globalization often have a downside, as international travel can now spread pandemics around the globe in a very short period of time.

As a description of the world we live in, the term "globalization" can be useful in highlighting common processes. Problems arise, however, when the term stands for a paradigm or overarching account of historical change. It does not always signify a paradigm, and even those who use the term do not agree on the overarching account. Indeed, much of the current debate concerns the bottom line: Is globalization good or bad? If it is deemed to be good, then the narrative is very different from when it is viewed as negative in its effects.[13]

Whether they think globalization is good for humanity or bad, proponents and critics of globalization can argue on this issue because they agree that there is a distinct process taking place and that its causes are in the first instance economic: the globalization of capital, especially of finance. Arjun Appadurai, one of the leading cultural theorists of globalization, repeats the contemporary common wisdom when he writes, "Globalization is inextricably linked to the current workings of capital on a global basis. . . . Its most striking feature is the runaway quality of global finance."[14]

According to this line of argument, capital markets and with them financial speculation are no longer constrained by national borders or even by industrial productivity. Since global capital is not fixed anywhere, it is "deterritorializing" in its impact; transactions no longer occur in a particular place. This deterritorialization, which some consider to define globalization, challenges the sovereignty of nation-states, which are after all built upon a notion of control over territory. Whether deterritorialization is the key feature of globalization or not, both the arguments for and against globalization consider the political, social, cultural, and even technological forms of globalization to be secondary or derivative from the primary factor of a globalizing economy.[15]

The more it operates as a paradigm, the more globalization talk posits the inexorability of the process. In an influential formulation, the British sociologist Anthony Giddens wrote, "Modernity is inherently globalizing," thus making globalization an inevitable accompaniment of modernization. Similarly, in *The Communist Manifesto* of 1848, Karl Marx and Friedrich Engels foresaw the inherently globalizing effects of capitalism: "The need of a constantly expanding market for its products chases the bourgeoisie over the entire surface of the globe. . . . In place of the old local and national seclusion and self-sufficiency, we have intercourse in every direction, universal inter-dependence of nations."[16]

Thus globalization as a paradigm asserts the inescapability of the process, the primacy of economics in driving it, and the desirability of research focused on economic factors. The research of the few historians who have tried to analyze globalization as a whole reflects this development. The Portuguese historian Cátia Antunes laid out the current models for historical research into globalization: Braudel's notion of total history, Immanuel Wallerstein's focus on world systems, and Andre

Gunder Frank's attempt to "reorient" thinking about globalization to pay greater attention to Asia, especially China.[17]

Unlike many others associated with the Annales school,
Braudel never limited his interests to France. After publishing
in 1949 his groundbreaking book on the entire Mediterranean
region (*The Mediterranean and the Mediterranean World in the
Age of Philip II*), he shifted his attention to the global history of
capitalism. *Civilisation et capitalisme* appeared in 1967 and was
later expanded into three volumes in 1979 under the general
title *Civilisation matérielle, économie et capitalisme*. Despite the
use of the word "civilization," the primacy of the economic in
general and capitalism in particular is clear. At the end of the
first volume, for example, Braudel casts capitalism as a unique
actor: "Capitalism could choose the areas where it wished and
was able to intervene, and the areas it would leave to their fate,
rebuilding as it went its own structures from these compo-
nents, and gradually in the process transforming the structures of others."[18]

Immanuel Wallerstein, an American sociologist, was so
taken by Braudel's work that he set up the Fernand Braudel
Center for the Study of Economies, Historical Systems, and
Civilizations at SUNY Binghamton and personally oversaw
its operation for nearly thirty years. Originally an expert on
Africa, Wallerstein insisted that every region of the world had
been part of a "world system" since the sixteenth century. In a
summary of his work published in 2004, he explained the connection to globalization: "The proponents of world-systems
analysis . . . have been talking about globalization since long
before the term was invented—not, however, as something
new but as something that has been basic to the modern

world-system ever since it began in the sixteenth century." The modern world system, he insisted, "is and always has been a *world-economy*. It is and has always been a *capitalist* world-economy."[19]

Andre Gunder Frank, a German American historian of economics of the same post-Braudel generation as Wallerstein, wrote his PhD dissertation on Ukrainian agriculture, but while teaching in Chile he published *Capitalism and Underdevelopment in Latin America* (1967), a key text in what was called "dependency theory." Reacting against modernization theory's view that all countries would pass through the same stages of development, dependency theory held instead that the rich nations kept poor nations in a dependent status in order to maintain their advantage of access to cheap labor and markets for manufactured goods.

Although dependency theory could fit with world-systems analysis in some respects, Frank believed that the world system went back much farther in time, to the spread of agriculture and writing ca. 4000 BC. This led him to an interest in Asia and especially China, because he believed that Wallerstein's analysis of the world economy was too Eurocentric. Indeed, he insisted that virtually all the previous attempts to compare the West and the Orient, from Marx and Weber to Braudel and Wallerstein, had been blinded by Eurocentrism. The title of his book, *ReORIENT*, made clear his intentions in this regard. But it is the subtitle of his book—*Global Economy in the Asian Age*—that is most relevant to my purposes here. Like Braudel and Wallerstein, Frank gives priority to economics.[20]

With its emphasis on the driving force of economic change, globalization as a paradigm has been as omnivorous as globalization is purported to be as a process; it gobbles up everything in its path. In this respect, the positions of Braudel, Wallerstein, and Frank, whatever the differences in interpretation between them, typify the globalization paradigm more generally. Globalization has incorporated two of the major paradigms of historical research, modernization and Marxism, and dramatically altered another, the paradigm of identity politics, while largely bypassing the fourth, the Annales school (despite Braudel's role).

Globalization, for many, is the new name for modernization, and Marxists now devote their attention to criticizing it as such rather than to developing an alternative. In the globalization paradigm, identity no longer derives from a fixed social category, such as ethnicity, or from a cultural construction, such as race. Globalization creates hybrid identities that burst the confines of the previous definitions and transform the conditions of identity politics. More than two decades ago Arjun Appadurai called attention to the development of "global ethnoscapes." The global movement of people, he predicted, would create new, previously unimagined, forms of identity. Tourists, refugees, guest workers, immigrants, and exiles would no longer be the exception to the rules of social identity. Their increasing importance would require new kinds of ethnography—a "transnational anthropology," according to Appadurai—that could capture the new forms of fluid, hybrid identities that crossed traditional borders. Sociologists now analyze "transnational identity politics," an effect created when "globalization hybridizes, particularizes, and postmodernizes culture and politics."[21]

The Annales school has remained relatively immune to the allure of globalization as a paradigm while promoting many varieties of transnational history, that is, studies of smaller "worlds" such as the Mediterranean, the Atlantic, or the Indian Ocean. Few followed Braudel's lead in analyzing the history of capitalism. In fact, most historians in France remain focused on particular nation-states, especially their own. Of some two thousand early-modern and modern historians in France surveyed in 2000, only twenty-nine were specialists in Russian or east European history; nineteen, in Chinese history; and fifteen, in Japanese history. The majority worked on France itself. France's relative tardiness in jumping on the globalization bandwagon has been deplored, yet it might turn out to have the advantages associated with "late" industrialization. It is easier to avoid the pitfalls when you can see what is coming.[22]

The absorption of three of the previous paradigms of historical research into one overarching globalization paradigm has two potentially troubling consequences: it shifts attention to macro-historical (worldwide) and especially macroeconomic trends, and it ensconces the assumption that economics shapes all other aspects of life. In short, the globalization paradigm reinstates the very suppositions that cultural theories had criticized, and thus potentially threatens to wash away the gains of the last decades of cultural history.

Much depends, however, on how globalization is studied, in particular whether it is approached from the top down or from the bottom up. Viewed from the top down, globalization is a process that transforms every part of the globe, creating a world system in Wallerstein's terms. Viewed from the bottom up, it is more likely to be a series of transnational processes in which the histories of diverse places become connected and interdependent. The shift in perspective does not lead to similar final results; on the contrary, the different perspectives yield divergent understandings of what globalization has been and is as a process.

The top-down perspective is one of world or global history. If the goal of historicizing globalization is, as world historian Jerry Bentley says, to focus on "large-scale processes that connect the world's many ostensibly distinct and discrete societies," then the international patterns of the exchange of goods and peoples almost inevitably take pride of place. If trade or commercial exchange is not foregrounded, then the movements of peoples and diseases are instead. The top-down perspective on globalization seems destined to draw historians' attention to macro-historical or systemic processes.[23]

The recent upsurge of interest in global or macro-historical points of view can be traced to various sources. The cacophonous discussion of globalization was bound to echo among historians who then sought to develop a history of the process that might answer some of the questions under debate, in particular, whether globalization took a fundamentally different form in recent decades. Dissatisfactions with cultural theories and with cultural historians' focus on the micro-historical fueled a reactive propensity for the macro-historical. As Patrick O'Brien remarks in an essay on global history, "There must be something more than an ambition to research and teach histories that offer what Dipesh Chakrabarty calls, 'a loving grasp of detail in search of the diversity of human life worlds.' " Finally, and not least, current events such as the "war on terror," the rise of China, and the global economic crisis have encouraged a global view.[24]

By abandoning the terrain of causal argument, cultural

theories left an opening for others to occupy, and those interested in the history of globalization or in a supposed return
to the "big questions" aimed to fill that causal void. In a book
titled *The Eastern Origins of Western Civilization*, for example,
John Hobson argued that the East ("which was more advanced
than the West between 500 and 1800") enabled, that is, caused
the rise of the West. His account of "oriental globalization"
tackles a long series of "big questions": "the myth of 1492" (the
idea that Europeans were unique in their capacity to discover
previously unknown lands); why Britain industrialized first
(it was the result of militarism, not technological innovation);
"the twin myths of the rational Western liberal-democratic
state and the great divide between East and West"; and so on.
Hobson aims to overturn the traditional account of the rise of
the West but proceeds from the same premise: that the rise of
the West is what needs explaining and can be explained only
from a top-down, economic perspective.[25]

The Peruvian sociologist Anibal Quijano offers an alternative anti-Eurocentric history of the origins of globalization. He
emphasizes the crucial role played by "America" (the Americas):
"America was the first modern and global geocultural identity.
Europe was the second and was constituted as a consequence
of America, not the inverse." Europe in its modern form took
shape on the backs of American Indians, blacks, and mestizos,
who brought to the table "advanced technology in mining and
agriculture" and such key ingredients as gold, silver, potatoes,
tomatoes, and tobacco. The Americas, not Europe, and not the
"East" for that matter, pulled the causal trigger.[26]

Quijano argues, moreover, that despite the end of direct
colonialism in most parts of the world, globalization still rests

on a "coloniality of power." The conquest of the Americas set up an enduring model of globalization that Quijano explicitly identifies with modernization. Globalization revolved around two interrelated axes: capitalism based on enforced labor, and "race," the biological codification of differences between the conquerors and the conquered. The rationale for the new system was Eurocentrism itself. Although Quijano argues that a cultural factor, race, plays an important role in globalization, he nonetheless subordinates it, first to political power (Eurocentrism arises from the fact of conquest) and then to the economic structures of global capitalism, which endure long after the end of the period of conquest. In the attempt to criticize Eurocentrism, he thus ends up making the "eurocentrification" of world capitalism seem inevitable. Economics triumphs once again.[27]

If cultural history was seen as too particularistic, too interested in idiosyncratic individuals and their micro-histories, and more interested in context than in causes, then the global and the macro-historical could be and were posited as superior alternatives. But the top-down perspective has some problems of its own. It takes globalization and the modern dominance of the West as givens and therefore prioritizes worldwide economic processes. It lends itself to developing causal answers to the supposed big questions but often poses the wrong big questions. As Sanjay Subrahmanyam argues, "We must abandon the developmental perspective that comes down to us with two fathers (Marx and W. W. Rostow), and which believes that the only question worth asking is that of Who Succeeded and Who Failed on the long road to modern industrial capitalism, from a list of modern nation-states."[28]

The importance assigned to worldwide processes and especially economics derives to some extent from the availability or lack of availability of data. It is much easier to develop quantitative indices of flows of goods and people than it is to trace the circulation of ideas or practices. As just one of countless examples that might be offered, a recent ambitious attempt to determine the influence of globalization on national systems of innovation in Asia and Europe begins by defining innovation in these terms: "new creations of economic significance, primarily carried out by firms." The "human development indicators" used for the study, based on contemporary data, are per capita GDP (gross domestic product) and life expectancy. It is easier to compare per capita income, for example, than it is to measure opportunities for personal development that take other, noneconomic forms. For earlier periods, economic indicators may be the only quantitative ones that are readily available. Just by virtue of enlarging the scale, then, the globalization paradigm favors economic and other structural explanations. Moreover, it often relies upon the very macroeconomic measures (GDP, GNP [gross national product]) that helped fuel Cold War "growthmanship" (i.e., our system is better than yours because it produces higher GNP).[29]

In fact, however, the bottom-up perspective is much more common among historians, if only because historical expertise depends on in-depth knowledge. Most global history is transnational (about the links established between two or more places not in the same state) or comparative (comparing two or more places) rather than truly global. Braudel, Wallerstein, and Frank have produced few emulators among historians. Braudel's three volumes on capitalism sought the economic origins of the modern world within Europe and offered richly descriptive material about ordinary life but no general thesis about globalization. Wallerstein and Frank put forth grand synthetic theories about the history of globalization but carried out no original research. Most historians, unlike the political scientist Hobson or the sociologist Quijano, have veered away from both total description and totally encompassing theories.

The bottom-up perspective offers a middle ground, seeking new evidence from which to build new generalizations rather than to test overarching theoretical models. Looking from the bottom up at globalization can accommodate various angles of vision as long as they cross over national boundaries. By deliberately looking across national boundaries, historians have rediscovered long-neglected transnational spaces such as borderlands, deserts, rivers, and oceans. When Braudel wrote about the Mediterranean, he focused almost exclusively on the littoral. He wanted readers to grasp the interconnections between the peoples living on the shores of the Mediterranean and its hinterland. The new oceanic approach reminds us that history is not just about landed territory but also about the bodies of water themselves. The more seas and oceans are emphasized, the less the nation-state as a landed territory seems the inevitable point of departure. Between 1990 and 1999, the *American Historical Review* published four reviews of books in which "ocean" figured in the title, but no articles. Between 2000 and 2009, it published seventeen such book reviews and five articles on the subject.[30]

A look at any of the journals dedicated to global history will show that the bottom-up perspective dominates. The March 2012 issue of the *Journal of Global History*, for example, includes articles on the financing of the United States and

Gran Colombia as new nations, Russian attitudes toward the Northwest Pacific in the eighteenth and early nineteenth century, early-nineteenth-century African American migration, and English associations in the Anglo world up until the 1930s. Only one article—on the use of national income estimates in global economic history—takes a worldwide view, and it questions the use of such estimates because they are biased in favor of European-style nation-states.[31]

Looking from the bottom up requires few prior assumptions. The historian need not presume, for example, that globalization is or always has been driven by economics. In an exemplary study of tobacco and chocolate in the Atlantic world, Marcy Norton shows how the Spanish learned to use them in the Americas from nursemaids, concubines, Indian healers, and market vendors. Returning colonists and sailors brought tobacco and chocolate back to Spain, but the commerce in those goods took off only at the end of the sixteenth century, a century after Columbus's maiden voyage. The first big shipments of chocolate were ordered by elite merchants and Catholic clergy who had spent time in the Americas. The story of tobacco is even more complex because many European governments tried to regulate and even monopolize it. Once plantation cultivation of tobacco spread throughout the Caribbean, smugglers, privateers, and shippers for all the European Atlantic nations competed furiously for the crops, establishing a taste for tobacco almost simultaneously in those nations. Before long, tobacco use expanded as well to the Middle East, Africa, India, China, and Japan.[32]

Consumption of tobacco and chocolate spread to Europe through a process of cultural syncretism. The increase in commerce did not follow immediately from conquest; it was made possible by changes in taste, and those changes took place under the influence of indigenous people, and in the case of chocolate, women in particular. The significance of these findings goes far beyond the world of early modern chocolate and tobacco, for, as Norton maintains, chocolate paved the way for coffee, and the two along with tea created a demand for sugar, for porcelain chocolate pots, and imitation Chinese teacups, and the like. With sugar came plantations and slavery. To buy slaves Europeans needed Indian textiles and cowry shells from the Maldives because those were the products preferred by African traders. In sum, the taste for chocolate and tobacco that developed in individual Spanish households in the Americas in the sixteenth century helped set in motion one of the most powerful early waves of globalization. The wave brought with it enormous economic changes, but its force can be comprehended only by paying attention to local cultural patterns and their changes over time: gender and race relations between conquerors and conquered peoples, class distinctions within Spanish and other European societies, and the ways people experienced changing tastes.

The bottom-up perspective has proved particularly fruitful in studying globalization in the early modern period (1500–1800). Improvements in shipbuilding and navigation enabled Europeans to travel across the globe, make contact with far-flung peoples, and establish various kinds of enduring links with them, often using brute military force and continuing coercion. Yet even while trade and military conflict took on global dimensions, communication across vast distances required considerable time, often several months. Correspondence and manuscript newsletters proved essential conduits of information about prices, commercial contacts, and currency exchange rates and have therefore provided invaluable historical evidence about the way globalization worked. The relatively low intensity of globalization in the early modern period makes it particularly amenable to study. Imagine trying to make sense of the billions of e-mails exchanged in global commerce in recent years, assuming that an investigator could be certain that e-mails—and not telephone calls or meetings in airport conference rooms—were the crucial means of interaction in present-day globalization. No such uncertainty attaches to the exchange of letters in the early modern period.

Studies of Sephardic Jews and of Armenians in Persia in the seventeenth and eighteenth centuries have drawn attention to networks of global trade that developed outside the circuits controlled by European conquerors and the great European merchant companies. Using more than thirteen thousand letters exchanged by a Sephardic Jewish family firm operating out of Livorno, Italy, Francesca Trivellato traces an astounding global trade of Mediterranean coral and Indian diamonds. The courier system of Julfan Armenians, studied by Sebouh Aslanian, enabled the Julfan merchants to trade in the Indian Ocean, the Mediterranean, northwestern Europe, and Russia, a truly incredible range for the time. Trivellato and Aslanian have shown how much trade depended on delicate cross-cultural transactions, on the willingness of family members to move far away, and on the exchange of correspondence, often over almost unimaginable distances. Diasporic communities, such as the Jews and Armenians, but also South Asians, Chinese, and Africans (not to mention Scots), have attracted particular interest because they carried and often still carry globalization in their baggage. They traveled, established new connections that they wove together with their old ones, and built globalization from the ground up, one letter, one sale, one relationship at a time.[33]

The bottom-up perspective makes it possible to revise the globalization paradigm in fundamental ways. Economic motivation need no longer be considered inherently primary, and even in the many instances where trade is the goal, it is clear that other factors—changing tastes, personal interactions, family ties, literacy, religious sensibilities—make global economic transactions possible. Moreover, the nation-state is not necessarily the relevant unit of comparison, an assumption often made only because most economic statistics were gathered by states in the modern period.

The case of ostrich feathers—those that adorned fancy ladies' hats in the late nineteenth and early twentieth century—is particularly instructive. Yiddish-speaking Lithuanian Jews who migrated from the Russian Empire to South Africa in search of economic and social opportunities served as key middlemen in the ostrich plume trade. They sold their merchandise to Jewish feather merchants in London. Some Sephardic Jewish family firms in London bought plumes that had been carried by trans-Saharan camel caravans to Tripoli and other North African cities. Still others came from Aden, where Yemeni Jews dominated the trade. The feathers were then reexported to Paris and New York. The pioneering historian of this trade, Sarah Stein, explains that it has been largely overlooked because it falls "in the as yet untheorized interstices of economic and cultural history." It can be traced only by following the local routes of supply and demand, however far-flung, not by interrogating state records or the records of one or two nations. Moreover, its rise and fall depended, as do all commodities, on changes in cultural patterns, in this case in ladies' fashions.[34]

It is not accidental that some of the most compelling historical studies of globalization have focused either on specific commodities such as chocolate, tobacco, diamonds, gold, textiles, mahogany, tea, and ostrich plumes or on particular ethnic networks such as Jews, Armenians, and South Asians. Only by tracing commodities and networks—the things exchanged and the people who exchange them—can the workings of globalization be truly understood. If deterritorialization is associated with globalization, then it is because things and people cross borders, not just going from one well-defined place to another (as in moving from one country to another) but also creating new kinds of interstitial spaces such as caravans, trade convoys, the haunts of pirates and smugglers, slave markets, and banks. New instruments of international interaction, such as currency exchanges and letters of credit, had to be invented to knit together those interstitial spaces. In short, deterritorialization and globalization do not happen willy-nilly through the operation of invisible institutions or processes; they occur because people act and interact.

This kind of bottom-up study effectively counters the notion that globalization is another name for modernization, that is, for the homogenization of the world through the circulation, absorption, and imposition of Western values. Globalization grew from a multitude of sources in the early modern period and beyond: Hindu merchants who traded in

Iran, Afghanistan, and Russian Central Asia; Julfan Armenians who traded in India, China, the Philippines, Russia, the Mediterranean (including the Ottoman Empire), and northwestern Europe; Muslims who plied the trans-Saharan route with gold, salt, leather, slaves, and manuscript books as well as their religion; the many peoples who worked one segment or another of the Central Asian caravan routes; and merchants passing Indian textiles through various hands to Africa and Europe—just to mention some of the examples from the early modern period.[35]

Europeans began to encroach on some though not all of these circuits, but even in the cases where Europeans did intervene, locals found new ways either of continuing old practices or of developing new niches for themselves. The West did not globalize the world on its own; adventurous and enterprising people across the world brought their various locales into greater interconnection and interdependence with each other. Since globalization is not therefore a uniquely Western creation, the globalization paradigm must be modified to take account of these multiple origins and processes. Globalization is not the same thing as modernization; globalization means interdependence (a two-way relationship), not simply the absorption of Western values (a one-way process). Non-Western histories and scholars are crucial to understanding the jointly constructed process of globalization.

With this bottom-up, more truly global perspective it is possible to counter some of the false assumptions of the globalization debates. Just as globalization is not the same thing as Westernization, so too the globalization of historical research need not mean that Eurocentric models of development will necessarily dominate. Modern science and the modern historical discipline may have taken root first in the West, but science and history are not Western in essence. Western geopolitical dominance has translated into Western dominance of science and to some extent history, but as the relations of power change, science and history will change too. In a study of global knowledge production in the twenty-first century, the British Royal Society found that between the periods 1999–2003 and 2004–2008, the share of the U.S. authorship of global publications dropped from the admittedly high level of 26 percent to 21 percent, while that of China rose from 4 percent to 10 percent, elevating China from sixth to second place over Japan, Great Britain, Germany, and France. The extent of change in such a short time frame is extraordinary and augurs similar if not greater changes in the future.[36]

Universal concepts—like globalization—are not inherently Western because they are universal. Walter Mignolo is among those who reject any universalist position because it can represent nothing other than the reiteration of the hegemony of Western civilization. He advocates "diversality, a project that is an alternative to universality and offers the possibilities of a network of planetary [worldwide] confrontations with globalization in the name of justice, equity, human rights, and epistemic diversality." The sentiments might be laudatory in their anti-Eurocentrism, but Mignolo fails to explain what authorizes the notions of justice, equity, human rights, and epistemic diversality. Are they not all universal claims in themselves, even the claim for diversality? Like many other critics of globalization, Mignolo takes it as a given and as a monolith.[37]

Endeavoring to get free from present-day U.S. political

hegemony or intellectual Eurocentrism should not lead to a refusal of all forms of social scientific or historical research, as some seem to suggest. Just because most of the social science disciplines (history, sociology, economics, anthropology) were first developed in Europe and spread outward from there, to among other places the United States, university-based research in these fields is not inherently "Western." Even Dipesh Chakrabarty, while criticizing "the discourse of 'history' produced at the institutional site of the university," fully participates in the research agenda of the university, which in this instance means writing critically about it. In the past, Western historians and social theorists did often use Europe as their touchstone for development, making invidious comparisons to non-Western cultures. They failed to appreciate until very recently, for example, the many varieties of history writing that could be found in non-Western cultures. This is precisely what the new research on early modern globalization succeeds in doing: showing how people living outside of Europe or in the interstices of European commerce, such as the Jews, have together created globalization on a worldwide canvas.[38]

Much research remains to be done from a cultural theory perspective on the emergence of globalization as a category of analysis. Why did "globalization" become a common term after the collapse of the Soviet Union? And why have so many assumed that globalization is first and foremost about deterritorialized capitalist markets? In answering such contemporary questions, the longer-term view of globalization is bound to be fruitful. Remarkable work has already been done on the early modern sources of globalization, but more remains to be done on this and on the different kinds of globalization. Hinduism, Buddhism, Christianity, and Islam all had globalizing influences with histories at least as long as those of capitalism and global commerce. Yet most recent scholarship has concerned the influence of globalization on religion, rather than the other way around. Connections and interdependence between regions are not established just through trade or military conquest, and though religion sometimes goes along with trade or military conquest, it does not always do so, as the spread of Buddhism through southeast, central, and eastern Asia shows. Moreover, these histories would demonstrate how religion, military conquest, trade, and politics are often intertwined, with now one, then another factor exercising the most influence.[39]

Similarly, the global spread, not to mention the local appeal, of nationalism in the nineteenth and twentieth centuries cannot be entirely, or even primarily, explained by economic developments. The study of nationalism has been revived in the last couple of decades by the injection of a cultural approach. Benedict Anderson pointed the way with his analysis of nationalism as an "imagined community," that is, a new form of deep attachment to people not in one's immediate kinship group. Anderson linked the emergence of nationalism to "print capitalism," which broke the power of the sacred scriptures of religious communities by facilitating the emergence of a mass readership of the vernacular languages. This spread of reading, especially in the form of novels and newspapers, in turn created a new sense of secular connection in which people could recognize their broader kinship with each other. When reading a newspaper, for instance, a person knew that others were reading the same paper at the same time, and this sense of simultaneity in secular time constituted the foundation of the newly imagined community of a nation. Although Anderson clearly intends to relate these developments to the growth of capitalism more generally, he puts the emphasis on the cultural elements; as he explains, he wants to argue that "nation-ness, as well as nationalism, are cultural artifacts of a particular kind."[40]

Others have pushed the cultural argument further, even while acknowledging Anderson's influence on their approach. In a series of pathbreaking books on Italian nationalism, for example, Alberto Mario Banti explicitly challenges the primacy of economic and social factors and draws attention to the role of emotional responses to patriotic expressions found in novels, histories, paintings, and songs (in other words, going beyond Anderson's novels and newspapers). People from very different social, political, religious, and regional backgrounds employed the same patriotic language of nationalism, which consisted of constantly recurring images and values such as kinship, sacrifice, and the trilogy of love, honor, and virtue. The ideals were old, but their connection to the nation was new. Banti emphasizes the affective, rather than the rational intellectual, responses to operas, poems, and paintings in order to explain the depth of the response to nationalism, its enduring quality, and its ability to entice even those who could not read, a group that comprised an important part of the population in a country such as Italy.[41]

Does nationalism foster or hinder globalization? It seems to do both. The nation-state spread as a global form in spurts between the revolt of the British North American colonies in

1776 and the present, and those outbreaks are now beginning to gain the attention they deserve. Revolts for independence in the 1820s (Latin America), 1918–1919 (Central Europe), 1947–1960s (decolonization), and 1990–1991 (former Soviet republics) are only just now being studied as transnational or regional clusters with powerful effects of their own on the forms of globalization. Moreover, the independence movement is far from over, even in the era of high globalization, and appears to be moving, paradoxically, in the direction of ever smaller units: East Timor, which gained its official independence in 2002, has a territory of 15,000 square kilometers (5,800 square miles), which makes it slightly bigger than Montenegro, which gained its independence in 2006, and bigger than only two of the fifty United States, Delaware and Rhode Island. The interconnectedness and interdependence of the world as a whole have only encouraged the desire of some for smaller rather than larger units of political affiliation. Many of the links between nationalism and globalization remain to be discovered, and the arrow of causality does not always fly from globalization to nationalism.[42]

Literature offers another promising possibility for reframing globalization in cultural terms. In her account of the "world republic of letters," Pascale Casanova prefers to talk of "internationalization," which she provocatively defines as "more or less the opposite of what is ordinarily understood by the neutralizing term of 'globalization.' " What she dislikes about the term "globalization" is the way it "suggests that the world political and economic system can be conceived as the generalization of a single and universally applicable model," such as modernization. She develops the notion of "world literary space" to counter the obsessive concern of most literary scholars with particular national literatures such as German literature, French literature, American literature, and Chinese literature. This world literary space has "its own laws, its own history, its specific revolts and revolutions," she maintains, but organizing it is the centrality of Paris. Paris's role as literary arbiter was first established in the sixteenth century in opposition to the prevailing influences of Italian humanism and the church in Rome. Over the centuries, this special role for Paris allowed writers from dominated societies or groups to make an international reputation. Thus by publishing in Paris, the Irish author James Joyce, the Czech Jewish writer Franz Kafka, and even the southern American writer William Faulkner could distinguish themselves from the dominant cultures in which they grew up and at the same time achieve a global artistic standing. The world literary space enabled them to escape the confines of particular nations.[43]

Although Casanova cites Braudel and the French sociologist Pierre Bourdieu as the major influences on her approach, she consistently emphasizes the relative autonomy of literary "capital" from economic and political determinations. It is not unrelated to geopolitical developments, but it does not follow them in lockstep. In short, the approach laid out by Casanova yields a very different picture of the processes of globalization, one in which cultural "capital" plays an important and sometimes paradoxical role. Paris did not become the literary world capital in the sixteenth century because it was the dominant world power, and it maintained its literary and intellectual position well into the twentieth century, even after France was defeated in World War II and subsequently lost many of its colonies. Economic dominance does not necessarily translate into other forms of superiority.[44]

These various approaches have highlighted many important aspects of globalization that were previously ignored, but they still fall short in one significant respect: they have yet to provide a coherent alternative paradigm of globalization. The proponents of a bottom-up approach have pointed, usually implicitly, to the defects of the current paradigm of globalization as a top-down, macroeconomic process, but they have not yet provided a replacement. Unlike the cultural theorists discussed in the preceding chapter, however, the historians employing bottom-up approaches to globalization have not shied away from questions of causality or even from the so-called big questions. They have asked, for example, why certain commodities stimulated new consumer demands when they did, and why certain groups or places played extraordinary roles in establishing globalizing networks. Instead of asking why some nation-states succeeded and others failed on the march toward modernization, they posed a better question: How did different peoples in various parts of the world, not necessarily identifiable by nation-state, contribute to globalizing markets, religions, politics, and culture? Now that these diverse approaches have shown their fruitfulness, other scholars, or even those who undertook these groundbreaking studies themselves, will be able to sift through the results and advance higher-level generalizations about the processes of globalization and how they have changed over time.[45]

THREE

RETHINKING SOCIETY
AND THE SELF

Globalization is not the only issue on the table. Two essential categories of history writing—society and the self—are undergoing top to bottom renovation. Unfortunately, historians have largely ignored these conversations, even though society and the self are foundational categories for any historical analysis. They are foundational in the sense that they make the writing of secular history possible, but because they are foundational, they are simply taken for granted rather than examined in sustained fashion. We think we know what society and the self are but would be hard pressed to give precise definitions.[1]

All four major paradigms of historical research in the postwar period—modernization, Marxism, the Annales school, and identity politics—assumed that the self and identity were shaped, if not entirely determined, by society, that is, by social conditions. At the same time, they nonetheless assumed that once individuals understood the ways in which they were socially conditioned, they would be able to act upon their knowledge and remake the social world. Modernizing rulers would develop their economies, Marxist workers would make revolution, and disadvantaged minorities would demand equal opportunity. But how can individuals entirely conditioned by social forces act in such a self-conscious fashion? This classic problem of human agency remained unresolved because the relationship between self and society was left unexamined.

Of the four paradigms, the Annales school proved to be something of an exception in this regard, even though Braudel paid little attention to the prospect for self-consciously enacted change and most Annales-school historians likewise emphasized the overwhelming impact of social and economic factors. In contrast, however, two of the original founders of the school, Bloch and Febvre, insisted on the interest of psychology for history. Bloch aligned his work with collective psychology, and Febvre went even further, urging historians to incorporate the findings of contemporary psychology into their historical investigations. With a life-long interest in individuals such as Luther and Rabelais, Febvre sensed that the self had to be entered into the equation in order to explain change. I will return to Febvre later in this chapter.

The cultural theories examined in the first chapter challenged the priority given to social conditioning but with paradoxical effects. While arguing for the relative autonomy of culture, cultural studies and postmodern theories often ended up giving even more determining power to culture, language, or discourse and virtually erasing the individual's capacity to act upon their knowledge. Foucault's rendition was especially troubling in this regard. Knowledge, in his view, did not produce truth or power; power produced knowledge and truth, and no one could escape the regime of that truth. Changes did occur in the regimes of power/knowledge/truth, but they were not brought about by anyone's conscious action; Foucault often cited the end of the eighteenth century as a period of transformation, but he never explained why change occurred at that time. It just happened.[2]

Society, understood in linguistic, discursive, or cultural terms by cultural theories, thus engulfed the self. The cultural critiques of selfhood drew upon an influential undercurrent in Western philosophy that emphasized the difficulties, uncertainties, and contradictions of selfhood. Developed by thinkers as diverse as Denis Diderot, Friedrich Nietzsche, and Sigmund Freud, it was then taken to new heights by Foucault, Derrida, and other postmodernists who questioned the very existence or at least salience of selfhood. Foucault maintained, for example, that the individual could not resist power because "the individual is an effect of power," not something existing outside of it.[3]

New ideas about the society-self connection are now emerging from an unlikely conjunction of influences. Globalization draws attention to the ways changing experiences of space and time alter social relations and with them concepts of the self and other. Studies of the non-West have cast doubt on the universality of Western conceptions of the self and society and of their linkages. Neuroscience and cognitive psychology are proposing new models of the self, thought, action, and social interaction. This chapter aims to combine elements from these sources to suggest alternative ways of thinking about society and the self. The relevance of these ideas, however, becomes apparent only when the power of previous conceptions is made clear. Society is the logical starting point because the conception of society took on new pertinence in the seventeenth and eighteenth centuries and became very much entwined with the process of secularization.

In 1987 Margaret Thatcher told the popular British magazine *Woman's Own* that there was "no such thing as society." In her memoirs she tried to explain this controversial remark by adding, "There are individual men and women and there are families." Thatcher could make these statements because society is an intellectual abstraction. She was, of course, willfully ignoring the fact that this particular intellectual abstraction had become part of common sense, at least in Western countries. She could do so because she was echoing the conservative political position in a debate that had by then spanned two centuries. That debate pitted those who emphasized the rights of autonomous individuals against the good of society, the supporters of Adam Smith against those of Jean-Jacques Rousseau, the adherents of liberalism against the advocates of socialism, and so on. Society, in that sense, was a loaded term, and she knew it.[4]

Before the seventeenth and eighteenth centuries, "society" referred to a connection, association, alliance, or partnership between individuals. Saints could find society in the mystical body of Christ, great nobles could join the king in a society of arms, and if you found enough friends to help you in a fight, you had a society. During the Enlightenment of the eighteenth century, society came into its own as something distinct from the state and from religion. It referred to the whole community and not some part of it; in short, society came to be seen as the secular organization of the nation around common laws, customs, or institutions. All of the *Oxford English Dictionary* references to "social" as concerning an institution or mechanism, referring to rank or status, or a theory concerned with the constitution of human society date from the mid-1700s or later. Similarly, French dictionaries give no definition for the adjective "social(e)" before 1762.[5]

The novelty of this sense of "social" was captured by the famous *Encyclopédie* of Diderot and Jean le Rond d'Alembert in 1765: "a word newly introduced into the language to designate the qualities that render a man useful in society and suited to the commerce between men." Crucial here is the insistence on commerce between men. "Society" and the "social" would now refer exclusively to life on earth separate from religious concerns. They would refer to the secular order.[6]

The changing meanings of the words "society" and "social" did not just reflect an underlying secularization; they were weapons in the struggle for secularization. In another place the *Encyclopédie* offered a definition of the word "philosopher," repeating a phrase that first appeared in an anonymous pamphlet of 1743: "Civil society is, in a manner of speaking, a divinity on earth for him." This was strong stuff and no doubt one of the reasons why the original pamphlet was published anonymously and the *Encyclopédie* itself was always in trouble with the authorities. Even though the definition maintains that society is a divinity only on earth for the philosopher, the use of the word "divinity" in this context had to raise hackles. Was not the king the closest thing to divinity on earth? Was not the clergy God's chief interpreter of what was divine and what was not? How could society be divine?[7]

In this way, over time and as a consequence of repeated conflicts, society was being established as the ground or frame of meaning. People would stop saying, or would say less often, that something happened because God willed it, and would say instead that the natural or social causes must be examined. Inequality, for example, would no longer be God-given, traditional, or just in the nature of things; it would require a social explanation, such as the one that Rousseau famously gave in his *Discourse on the Origin and Foundations of Inequality among Men* (1755). Religion was being supplanted as the ultimate frame of reference; society and the social were taking its place.

Enlightenment writers were usually reluctant to push this position to its furthest possible conclusion: materialism and atheism. The entry in the *Encyclopédie* defining the philosopher continues in a more sober vein: "[The philosopher] burns incense to it [civil society], honors it by his probity, by an exact attention to his duties and by a sincere desire not to be an unuseful or burdensome member of it." Enlightenment adherents, for all their criticisms of the status quo, wanted to be seen as men of honor and probity, not as immoral atheists and materialists. Society might be a god on earth for the Enlightenment, but its worship on earth would not lead to moral breakdown: "The philosopher is therefore a respectable man who always acts with reason and who combines his reflective and correct mind with a sociable lifestyle and friendly qualities."[8]

The full consequences of society displacing religion as the framework of meaning emerged only in the early twentieth century, when Durkheim analyzed religion itself in social terms. In *The Elementary Forms of the Religious Life* (1912), the founding father of sociology pronounced, "God and society are one and the same thing." Society creates gods (and not the other way around) since society "has everything it needs for awakening in minds the sensation of the divine through the effect that it exercises on them." The French Revolution provided an especially interesting example for Durkheim of "this aptitude of society for erecting itself as god or for creating gods." Although the Cult of the Supreme Being and the Cult of Reason had only an ephemeral existence in the French Revolution, the exception nonetheless proved the rule. All religion was simply society expressing its inner logic.[9]

Few eighteenth-century thinkers would have accepted Durkheim's assimilation of God to society (and many people, needless to say, still do not). The grounding of society in human needs and desires did not necessarily make the supernatural superfluous. Rousseau, like many others, argued for the necessity of religion. In his "Profession of Faith of the Savoyard Vicar" in *Emile* (1762), he laid out the case for a kind of Christianized deism. Still, even in the case of Rousseau's argument for religion, we can see how the social is becoming gradually established as the ground of meaning; increasingly, religion is justified in terms of its social utility. Thus we do not have to follow Durkheim to his ultimate conclusion to see the power of the ascription of meaning to the social.

Secularization in the West went hand in hand with the belief that society institutes itself, whether through a social contract or some other means. Meaning then becomes immanent in social relations and is created by the social bonds themselves, not derived from a supernatural, transcendent source. Yet secularization does not inevitably entail the elimination of religion. Rather, it causes the compartmentalization of religious belief. In a secularized society, religion is relegated to the private sphere, to the realm of individual or family choice. Believers may hold that the truths of their religion are absolute, but in a secular society they are not meant—at least in principle—to force others to hold the same beliefs.[10]

Society is not only an intellectual abstraction; it is also a lived experience of shared rules, constraints, and possibilities for participation. Although society in this sense has always existed, it was not always an object of conscious examination or conceptualization in the way it came to be in the eighteenth century and afterward. The term "social science," for example, appeared for the first time in French in 1789, at the beginning of the French Revolution. Society became more visible as new spaces were created between the individual and his or her family on one side and the state on the other; these spaces are often called "civil society."[11]

New kinds of voluntary associations that appeared in the late seventeenth and in the eighteenth century made civil society more textured and conspicuous. Coffeehouses proliferated after a Middle Eastern Jewish entrepreneur opened the first one at Oxford in 1650. London alone housed eighty-two coffeehouses by 1663 and no less than five hundred by 1700. Many of them played on their association with the exotic (coffee came from the Middle East), using "Turk," "Black," "Saracen," "Sultan," "Smyrna," or "Africa" in their names. As coffeehouses and cafés spread across Europe from west to east, other new social forms popped up: daily newspapers and periodicals, Freemason lodges, salons, public music concerts and art exhibitions, local learned societies, debating clubs, reading societies, and finally political clubs. They swelled in number, giving people things to do and see beyond their family homes and parish churches.[12]

The more the space of the social thickened, the more people began to comment and write about it. Enlightenment thinkers started the process of systematizing thought about society. The Scottish moral philosophers Adam Ferguson and John Millar, for example, wrote histories of the development of civil society, tying its rise to the evolution of mankind from barbarism to civilization embodied by "the modern European nations." "Civil society" went on to a brilliant if controversial career, serving as the marker of Western modernity, the necessary precursor to democratic government, and, in the 1980s and afterward, the designation for the groups who organized to oppose repressive states.[13]

"Civil society" required more specificity when the nineteenth century brought industrialization and urbanization to Western countries. Politics no longer pitted civil society against the ruler but rather different groups within civil society against each other for control over governments now legitimized by their representation of the nation. In the nineteenth century, consequently, class emerged as a category of social distinction. The "social question"—fears of growing social division—began to occupy novelists (Balzac used the phrase in 1846) and reformers. The social sciences began to take shape as distinct disciplines.

According to the British Marxist and cultural critic Raymond Williams, "the modern structure of *class* in its social sense" began to be built up only at the very end of the eighteenth century. "Higher classes" and "middle" and "middling classes" appeared first as English terms in the 1790s. "Working classes" appeared in 1815, "class consciousness" even later. As for the social sciences, "sociology," for example, appeared in English for the first time in 1842 in reference to the work of the French philosopher Auguste Comte, who had used the term repeatedly in his *Cours de philosophie positive* of 1830. "Socialism" appeared in the mid-1830s. At the end of the nineteenth century, university departments of sociology began to appear, first in the United States and then in France and Germany. In short, the terminology, as well as the experience, of society and the social went through a long process of differentiation.[14]

A complete history of the increasing visibility of society cannot be given in a few paragraphs. What matters is that such a history can be told. The notion that the social is the ground of meaning has a history, and it is therefore not a universal or timeless truth. It is in fact a peculiarly Western truth tied to the rise of natural science and of representative government from the late seventeenth century onward. The discoveries of Isaac Newton and his predecessors gave eighteenth-century Enlightenment thinkers the confidence that science could be applied to society and social relations. Over the course of the eighteenth century, educated people in western Europe and the British North American colonies increasingly came to believe that government should represent civil society.

The enduring influence of the nineteenth- and twentieth-century social theories of Marx, Weber, Durkheim, Freud, and Foucault testifies to the power of this conception. They disagreed about how the social operated, and succeeding theorists often built their positions on refutations of their forbears. For Marx, the key was changing modes of production; for Weber, concerns about status; and for Durkheim, increasing specialization of social roles. For Freud, the social worked through individual psychic repression, while in Foucault's view, discursive regimes structured the social world. Despite these fundamental differences, they all believed that the social was the ground of meaning.[15]

This conception of society has not lost its power for making sense of human action. Just as natural science, with its laboratories, university departments, research centers, and peer-reviewed journals, has been emulated and imitated in all countries of the world, so too the humanities and social sciences as developed in the West have had great influence on the cultures of knowledge of the rest of the world. The schedule of degree courses at the University of Delhi and the list of schools at Shanghai University look very much like their counterparts at Oxford University and the University of Pisa. The similarity has helped promote globalization, perhaps, but it is not simply a confirmation of the effects of globalization. Universities are not similar because the modalities of capitalism demand that they be so. The deterritorialization of capital could have worked just as well, perhaps even better, with universities in some countries and not others. Indians, Chinese, and other peoples have established Western-style universities because they perceived Western cultures of knowledge to be linked to the technological, military, and economic superiority that Western countries established in the nineteenth century. Moreover, cultures of knowledge can have an economic influence; the World Bank now explicitly holds that knowledge is "the key engine of growth" in the world today. But today's "knowledge economies" are as much cultural as they are economic.[16]

The continuing explanatory power of the social in our time should not blind us to the fact that it has not always been so, is not so for everyone, and may not continue to be so. This is where globalization comes in. Globalization, even if its nature and timing are still very much up for debate, has the salutary effect of challenging our most basic assumptions about space and time and therefore about society. The functioning of society depends on the regulation of space and time. Whether we consider Louis XIV's elaborate rules for who could sit close to him at a court event or the temporal and spatial organization of the life of a contemporary Yemeni dockworker, it is evident that temporal rhythms and spatial grids are crucial elements in the construction of any social order. Insofar as globalization alters the experience of space and time, it also affects the experience of social relations and with them the very notion of society. If society is defined, as it was in the *International Encyclopedia of the Social Sciences* in 1968, as "a relatively independent or self-sufficient population characterized by internal organization, territoriality, cultural distinctiveness and sexual recruitment," then globalization either erases society or at least points to the need for a new understanding of how it works.[17]

Society, the frame of social relations and conditions, has usually been identified with the nation-state. Social scientists speak of French society, Brazilian society, or Vietnamese society. They study conflicts, wage gaps, or differences in life expectancy between groups or classes within one state, and if they examine struggles for power, they assume that power resides in local, regional, or national institutions. With globalization, however, society no longer sits so comfortably within the boundaries of the nation-state, if indeed it ever did. Wage gaps in the United States, for example, depend as much on international differences in pay as they do on social conflicts at home. Power in Mexico does not depend just on Mexican voters; it is shaped by the flow of drugs, arms, and people across the borders. What matters then is the international flow and network of people, commodities, and information. In short, society can no longer be identified with the nation-state because social relations no longer fit within the nation-state's boundaries.[18]

The questions now being raised about society as a category do not lessen its significance, as Thatcher might have wished to do, but they do suggest the increasing unsettledness of the concept. The boundaries of society are up for discussion, and not just whether they coincide with those of nation-states. Also at issue are the boundaries between human society and nature and those between humans and nonhumans, whether animals or inanimate objects. In the seventeenth and eighteenth centuries, society was conceptualized as a space of autonomy from the demands of religion and from rulers claiming absolute, divinely justified authority. Society represented an entirely different kind of legitimacy, one tied to the inherent nature of humans and their evolving institutions, rather than to transcendental or supernatural forces. As a result, much discussion of society from the eighteenth to the twentieth centuries took the form of debates over human nature and the consequences for it of changes that were occurring in the organization of society. Those debates are now taking different forms, especially when humans are viewed in a much longer time frame and as players in a larger world rather than as masters of it.

When viewed in the perspective of a deep history of evolution, going back millions of years, far beyond the threshold of written history, human nature itself appears in a different light. Although evolutionary biologists and anthropologists debate the significance of this long-term perspective for the present day, at the very least historians might be reminded not only of the common origins of humans in Africa but also of the kinship of humans with animals.

Our view of society would be sharpened if we paid more attention to the reciprocal relationship between biology and culture rather than viewing them as infused by entirely separate logics. Historian Daniel Smail has argued for a "new neurohistory" that would amalgamate biological and cultural approaches, take into account the deep history of humankind, and as a consequence, rethink some of the presumptions that historians customarily make. By taking the long or deep view, he suggests, we might be able to avoid some of the long-standing prejudices against black Africa that animated many accounts of the emergence of civilization from the white Middle East. Smail wants historians to pay attention to evolutionary accounts, but he also wants them to consider how culture and history might modify such accounts. Darwin held that the social instinct was an evolutionary trait in both humans and animals that developed through natural selection. But we can still ask how the instinct for the social changed over time, even in the centuries closer to our own. For example, somatic responses to stimuli such as rage or fear are wired into the brain, but just which stimuli triggers them varies culturally and historically.[19]

Our view of society might also improve if we considered the history of the efforts of humans to differentiate themselves from animals. How do those distinctions vary over time and geographical space? In her pathbreaking book on English attitudes toward animals, historian Harriet Ritvo begins with an arresting example: the hanging of a woman for bestiality in London in 1679 alongside her canine partner in crime. In 1906 the American linguist and historian Edward Payson Evans published an extraordinary account of the criminal prosecution and capital punishment of all sorts of insects and animals in the course of western European history. Among the cases clustered in particular in the fifteenth and sixteenth centuries was the execution of a number of pigs that had killed children. Lawyers were named to defend rats that destroyed crops and insects that devastated vineyards. Lengthy arguments were heard about the rights of animals and insects, for according to Genesis they had been created before man. If God had commanded them to be fruitful and multiply, then according to their defenders they were only exercising their legitimate rights when they took up their abode in the crops or vines of humans.[20]

Evans celebrated the end of such legal proceedings as a victory over "the childish disposition to punish irrational creatures," yet as Ritvo argues, the end of such practices had another, more disturbing implication: animals became the property of their human owners, and they were now completely subordinate to humans. They might be objects of affection, and in the nineteenth century societies would be set up for their protection from cruelty, but animals no longer exercised agency of their own. Any sense that animals participate in the construction of human society was lost.[21]

This supposedly modern attitude toward animals as

objects for human use is now being called into question. A "World Declaration on Great Apes" drawn up by the Great Ape Project, an association of those interested in the rights of great primates, specifies that all human beings, chimpanzees, bonobos, gorillas, and orangutans should enjoy the right to life, the protection of individual liberty, and the prohibition of torture. Research on animal and human genomes has shown that humans share about 99 percent of their DNA with chimpanzees and bonobos. It is especially noteworthy that though the research is most often motivated by the desire to pin down the distinctiveness of humans, it frequently ends up underlining genetic similarities as much as it does differences.[22]

Just as humans are not the only ones with rights, so too society is perhaps not an exclusively human construction. Did humans domesticate dogs, or did dogs domesticate humans? Archaeological studies of Siberia have shown that hunter-gatherers of the early Neolithic (ca. 5000 BC) sometimes buried dogs in their cemeteries, shared their food with them, and probably shared tasks with them too. Dogs may well have played an important role in their cosmological beliefs. In any case, these people obviously considered at least some dogs to merit the same respect due humans.[23]

Questions about animals are closely related to the issues posed by environmental history. The natural environment is not just something we humans act upon; it is something we live with, in, on, as well as off of. We reshape the environment, we build upon it, but increasingly it has become apparent that we also "owe" something to it, that is, that we have a social relationship with it. It is not inert, a formlessness waiting for human intervention to give it meaning. As German historian Dorothee Brantz remarks, historians of the environment have been quick to acknowledge that nature is culturally constructed (that nature is a cultural category, not a natural one), but they "seem to be very reluctant to consider the reverse, namely that nature also influences the construction of culture and social life." Brantz urges historians to engage more closely with concepts of space, place, landscape, and environment, recognizing, for instance, that even cities, man-made objects par excellence, are completely tied up with nature's processes. Cities require water, air, and green spaces to be inhabitable. She sees space as providing a conceptual link between nature and culture because it is at once physical and sociocultural. It also provides an opportunity to move beyond cultural theories' emphasis on discourse. Whereas cultural theories might pay attention to the discourses about space, environmental historians analyze its actual use, the interface it provides between humans and nature, and the ways nature talks back.[24]

We ignore the agency of the natural world at our peril. When Hurricane Katrina struck New Orleans in August 2005, the storm surge breached the man-made levees and flooded 80 percent of the city. The event shocked public opinion, not so much because of the loss of life (the toll of some fifteen hundred dead was much lower than that of many major earthquakes in China or Iran, for example), but because of the inability of humans to protect the city. Did the failure to prevent erosion of surrounding wetlands worsen the impact of the natural disaster? Had the U.S. Army Corps of Engineers, responsible for building levees for over a century, used inadequate data or outmoded techniques? It turns out that humans do not control or manipulate nature as thoroughly as sometimes thought.

Climate change, which may or may not have been responsible for Katrina's fury, brings such issues into even clearer
relief. Dipesh Chakrabarty argues that climate change threatens the very foundation of history by its potential to disrupt
the continuities between past, present, and future. Climate
change undercuts the age-old separation between natural history and human history. It even undermines some of the core
assumptions of environmental historians who have led the
way in attempting to reconnect natural and human history. In
particular, it challenges the assumption that humans are first
and foremost biological agents whose microbes, for instance,
have powerful effects all on their own. When exchanged, as
microbes were in the New World, large populations were
wiped out. Humans must now be seen as geological agents too,
capable of destroying the earth's environment. Chakrabarty
calls upon the kind of deep historical perspective proposed by
Smail to make the menace comprehensible. People must begin
to think and act as a species, and yet it is virtually impossible
to experience oneself as part of a species. Will the potential
catastrophe of climate change induce species identification,
and what will the consequences be for our notion and experience of the social? At the very least, historians must recognize
that the boundary between the human (including the social)
and nature is far more porous than previously thought.[25]

The boundaries between humans and their objects have
also come into question. The computer and the microchip have
made this boundary seem particularly unstable. Computers can
be taught to think like humans, and human minds are increasingly thought of as information processors. Microchips can
already be implanted in animals and humans to store informa-

tion, and various artificial devices can be implanted in humans to replace body parts (hips, knees, intraocular lenses), raising the prospect of microchips that might someday enable the paralyzed to walk and the like. Without going as far as some commentators who argue that these developments obliterate any sense of human agency, it is clear that transplants raise questions about the nature of individual and even human identity.[26]

The relationship of humans with the objects they make has always had effects that escape conscious notice. The spread of clocks, first in public spaces in the fifteenth and sixteenth centuries, and then of domestic clocks and watches in the eighteenth century, produced a slow revolution in the experience of social life itself. Time became full of events, systematic calculations became part of daily life, numbers and numeracy became more vital, and a new common sense that involved time emerged. Increasing temporal precision went hand in hand with greater social density. Clocks encouraged new forms of cognition not originally envisioned by their makers. Clocks, in short, changed the nature of human beings. Objects are not just manipulated by the humans who create them; they have effects of their own on their creators.[27]

If the boundaries of the social are up for debate, then it is not surprising that questions are being asked as well about the limits of social explanation. Since the idea that the social was the ground of meaning arose only in the modern period and first in the West, how should historians treat people from previous times and other places who do not share this assumption? They cannot simply be written off as traditional, backward, or primitive. Religion poses the greatest dilemmas in this regard because in the West the autonomy of society and social explanation itself emerged from the confrontations with the power of religion, the church, and the link between throne and altar. Indeed, "religion" as a category comes out of these same confrontations. In his presidential address to the American Academy of Religion in 1983, Wilfred Cantwell Smith influentially argued that " 'religion' is a secularist notion, a conceptual element in that particular worldview," and moreover, that it is one that "distorts what it seeks to illuminate" because it posits religion as an add-on, just another element in social identity. Smith was not content to argue for the incommensurability of frameworks of meaning and against the reduction of religion to social factors; instead he concluded that "modern secularism is an intellectual error" that had to be overturned as soon as possible in favor of greater appreciation of "transcendence." It is nonetheless possible to separate the insight about religion as a Western category from the solution proposed by Smith.[28]

Postcolonial scholars like Chakrabarty have been endeavoring to do just that. Chakrabarty recognizes that some kind of translation between religious claims and "understandable (that is, secular) causes" is "inevitable and unavoidable," but he still wants to put pressure on the act of translation, or what I am calling here social explanation. He asks, "How do we conduct these translations in such a manner as to make visible all the problems of translating diverse and enchanted worlds into the universal and disenchanted language of sociology?" We cannot overcome the incommensurability of frameworks of meaning. Indeed, we should keep that incommensurability in mind. And we should also recognize the limits that social explanation necessarily runs up against, even while utilizing its continuing power. The difficulty of these issues has not put off the increasing number of historians interested in the history of religion. According to the American Historical Association, religion eclipsed cultural history as the single largest category of thematic interest of historians in 2009, though in many regards the two fields are not all that distinct.[29]

These various ways of contesting the boundaries of society and of social explanations do not add up to one neat new package of thinking about society. All of the presuppositions about society have been called into question, even the representations of time and space. The modern discipline of history depends on certain distinctive representations of space and time. The maps used by historians rely on modern Western forms of visual abstraction including a bird's-eye (or God's-eye) view in which the entire space is visible with no one privileged point of view. The common Western periodization of history categorizes time into prehistory, ancient, medieval, and modern epochs. The applicability of these forms to other cultures is up for debate, as are the hidden limitations or distortions they might impose on contemporary historical writing. In sum, the concept of society will now have to be rebuilt from the ground up.[30]

If the meanings and boundaries of society are now in question, what can be ventured about the self, which for decades has been cast as the weaker partner in the society-self match? The self was not always considered an automatic by-product of social conditions, for the ideals and practices of individual autonomy emerged hand in hand with the notion of society and new social practices during the eighteenth century. Adam Smith and Rousseau might have been concerned, each in his own way, with the tensions between society and self, but they would not have been able to have the discussion without the simultaneous appearance of the opposing poles.

Society, the individual self, and secularization were closely linked together in the eighteenth century. Society was the space of autonomy or freedom from the demands of authoritarian rulers claiming a transcendental ground of legitimacy. Its emergence as a concept and set of practices implied a challenge to that transcendental ground of legitimacy, whether in the form of the divine right of kings or the biblical link between the father's authority and the authority of the Crown. In other words, the increasing attention to society propelled secularization by undermining the supernatural grounds of authority. Society authorized itself. It was self-regulating, though not always with the greatest success.

Over the course of the eighteenth century, society came to be seen as composed of individuals and not just families and status groups such as the nobility, the clergy, or the many guilds of professions and occupations. As a consequence, government was increasingly seen as representing individuals, especially individual property owners, rather than status groups. Thus, the first issue in the French Revolution of 1789 was whether the Estates-General should vote by order (clergy, nobles, Third Estate) or by "head" (by individual deputy). Voting by head won out. The nation was to be composed of individual citizens, not differentially privileged status groups. In short, society's autonomy from authoritarian rule was not enough; individuals had to be as autonomous as possible from the pressures of their families and communities as well.

The appearance of the language of natural rights or "the rights of man" in the various eighteenth-century revolutions

was made possible by this new emphasis on individual autonomy and the secularization of the foundations of government.
Rights inhered in the person, and governmental legitimacy
depended on the protection of them. By the end of the nineteenth century Durkheim could argue that human rights were
becoming the civic religion of an increasingly secularized
society. But the correlation between the needs of society and
the rights of the individual was always problematic. It still is
today.[31]

Even as human rights became more and more prominent
as a political, cultural, and moral doctrine in the twentieth
century (to make another very long story short), the social
paradoxically began to trump the individual self in many
domains of thought. Practical as well as philosophical reasons contributed to the diminishing of the self. Feminists and
race theorists, for example, hold the conviction that individual
behaviors and identities are shaped by social and cultural factors because they want to argue against biological (natural or
so-called essentialist) explanations for gender or racial distinctions. Women were not subordinated to men because of their
nature but rather because of their lack of education, inadequate
access to opportunities, unequal pay for equal work—in short,
because of prejudice created by a social and cultural order.
Similarly, whites did not gain power over blacks by virtue of
their superior racial characteristics. Having political and cultural power, whites proclaimed their preordained dominance
by championing racism. If gender and race are categories created by discourse (that is, socially constructed), then they are
historical and subject to change. At the same time, however,
individual identity and action are submerged in a pool of social

and cultural determinations. The individual seems incapable of resisting social control.[32]

The autonomous self that emerged hand in hand with society in the eighteenth century now is in danger of complete eclipse. Joan Scott's position can be taken as exemplary because it has had such wide influence and because it makes the case in no uncertain terms: "We need to attend to the historical processes, that through discourse, position subjects and produce their experiences. It is not individuals who have experience, but subjects who are constituted through experience." As with Foucault, there is nothing coming from inside the self that shapes the social. Moreover, Scott insists, historians, social scientists, and literary critics who try to base their work on the unexamined experiential claims of individual selves end up facilitating, rather than dismantling, these effects of social construction. They inadvertently reproduce the dominant ideology. Only one conclusion is possible, she argues: "Subjects are constituted discursively and experience is a linguistic event."[33]

Scott at least takes seriously the problem of subjectivity or interiority, which is more than can be said for most contemporary historians who pay little or no attention to what constitutes the self. This allergy among historians to talk of the self is actually a relatively recent development, however. The founding fathers of social theory and even of social history showed great interest in psychosocial linkages. Durkheim and Weber and social historians such as the Annales-school founder Lucien Febvre believed that social analysis required both social and psychological dimensions. Around 1940, Febvre and the German sociologist Norbert Elias laid out influential but very different models for psychosocial historical analysis.

Elias, writing in exile in the 1930s, made the first sustained effort to combine Freud's insights with those of a sociological and historical perspective. In *The Civilizing Process* (1939) he traced the history of manners in order to show that the self had a history. Elias maintained that the notion of a self-contained individual—a self with invisible walls separating it from others—had gradually developed only since the fourteenth century. Over time, self-control increased as the threshold of shame lowered. Blowing your nose into your hand, eating with your hands out of a common bowl, and sleeping in a bed with a stranger became disgusting or at least unpleasant. Violent outbursts of emotion and aggressive behavior became socially unacceptable. These changes in manners signaled the advent of the self-enclosed individual, whose boundaries had to be respected in social interactions. In a new preface appended in 1968, Elias confirmed that he intended to show the long-term connection between control over affect in individuals and the increasing differentiation and integration of social structures (i.e., modernization).[34]

Elias's developmental narrative took the Middle Ages as its point of departure and depicted that time period as infantile in its emotional expressions. People at the time, he argued, vented their emotions more violently and directly and had therefore fewer psychological nuances and complexities in their ideas about conduct. Intense piety, violent feelings of guilt, sudden outbursts of joy and hilarity, boastful belligerence, and a taste for cruelty went hand in hand with what Elias explicitly terms "childish" expressions and forms of behavior. Elias's pejorative depiction of the Middle Ages revealed the downside of a developmental historical psychology: the attempt to elaborate on the parallel between individual and broader cultural or social development encouraged scholars to classify earlier times as infantile, childish, or immature. This remains one of the most pressing problems in historicizing psychoanalytic or psychological insight.[35]

The other major model for a psychosocial history was non- if not anti-psychoanalytic. In 1941 Febvre advocated the study of sensibility, that is, of the emotions and their expression or what he called *la vie affective*. Emotions have both individual psychological and social dimensions, Febvre insisted, and historians could benefit from closer reading of the psychologists. Because he considered emotions fundamental to social life, he advised his fellow historians to investigate the history of love, death, joy, and cruelty. But he also considered emotions deeply problematic because of the potential for atavistic mob behavior, so evident to him in the rise of fascism in his own time. Like Elias but with much less elaboration, Febvre advanced a developmental schema or "longlasting drama": "the more or less slow repression of emotional activity through intellectual activity." Febvre was influenced by the child psychologist Henri Wallon, who argued that childhood development took place through a series of stages of antagonism between affectivity and intellection, with intellection eventually winning out. Yet Wallon did not think that individual development was entirely linear, and in any case his emphasis on the emotions as the foundation for intersubjectivity (sharing between minds) foreshadowed important elements of contemporary research into the way cognition works.[36]

Few historians heeded the challenges set forth by Elias and Febvre. The Annales school focused on the social side in the "history of mentalities." It employed no particular psychological theory or approach and remained largely confined to the study of conscious and collective beliefs and prejudices. French historians examined the history of death, for example, but they usually looked at funeral rites and cemeteries rather than at individual feelings. Similarly, some French historians followed Elias's lead in studying civility and court society in the seventeenth century, but showed interest only in the social dimension of his analysis. Even Alphonse Dupront, one of the leading French practitioners of historical psychology, described his approach as closest to the social history of ideas.[37]

On the other hand, the few self-proclaimed "psychohistorians," those who tried to apply an explicit psychological or psychoanalytical model in their research, ignored Elias and Febvre and with them the social dimension altogether. For the most part, psychohistorians tied their fortunes to an unnecessarily ahistorical version of Freudianism, insisting, unlike Elias, that the truths of psychoanalysis were universal and timeless. When the founder of the *Journal of Psychohistory* claimed that "the relationship between history and psychohistory is parallel to the relationship between astrology and astronomy," he made the enterprise seem risible to most historians. Even psychoanalytically minded historians have been loath to associate themselves in any way with psychohistory.[38]

Historians' antagonism to psychological approaches derived in part from their political objections to the conclusions of the field known as crowd psychology, an important precursor of present-day social psychology. Although not an academic social science, crowd psychology exercised great influence on literature, the social sciences, and history at the end of the nineteenth century and continued to enjoy considerable prestige well into the twentieth. The best-known practitioner of the genre was Gustave Le Bon, an independent scholar with many connections to the political elite in France. His book *The Crowd*, first published in French in 1895, drew on the work of several French and Italian investigators of mass behavior. Le Bon argued that the individual in a crowd suffers a kind of hypnosis in which he becomes "an automaton who has ceased to be guided by his will." On becoming part of an organized crowd, "a man descends several rungs in the ladder of civilization" and becomes a "barbarian." Crowds have the characteristics of "beings belonging to inferior forms of evolution," which Le Bon equated with "women, savages, and children." Le Bon believed that crowd psychology explained the "pathologies" of modern society such as workers' strikes and riots and especially socialism.[39]

Given the affinity of crowd psychology with extreme right positions—Mussolini claimed to have read Le Bon's book several times, and Hitler may well have used it as a source for *Mein Kampf*—it is hardly surprising that the pioneers of social history in the 1950s and 1960s distanced themselves from this kind of psychological analysis. George Rudé, for example, explicitly contradicted Le Bon in his studies of the crowd in history. The Parisian crowds of the French Revolution were composed, Rudé insisted, of hardworking, ordinary family men of the neighborhood who wanted cheap and plentiful food above all else. In short, they acted out of conscious, rational motives, not out of irrational mob psychology. Rudé insisted that crowd behavior was best explained in sociological, not psychological, terms.[40]

An exception to the rule may underline its general validity. The one section in Thompson's influential *Making of the English Working Class* that used psychological categories was the one on Methodism, a revivalist offshoot of the Protestant Church of England that spread rapidly in England and the United States in the late eighteenth and early nineteenth century. Why were so many working people willing to submit themselves to what Thompson termed "psychic exploitation"? Methodist "hysteria" arose in reaction to the defeat of supporters of the French Revolution in England, Thompson insisted. Religion was a kind of safety valve for suppressed revolutionary aspirations. Good crowds were never subject to psychologizing, it seems, only bad (in this case, politically passive) ones.[41]

The rise of social history therefore entailed a rejection of most forms of psychological analysis. Social explanation seemed to validate the motives of ordinary people, whereas psychological interpretations effectively censured them. Foucault did not have the same aims—he was not interested in validating the motives of the crowd—yet his approach, too, worked against any psychological explanation. Although he was deeply concerned with the construction of individuality through various kinds of disciplinary practices, his focus was on bodies, not selves. In fact, he denied that individual consciousness was even involved: "If power gets into the body, it isn't because it has been interiorized in people's consciousness." Bodies are molded by institutions such as prisons without the mind knowing.[42]

Influenced by Foucault, cultural historians, and especially gender historians, have produced groundbreaking work on the discourses and practices regarding the body. Discipline in schools, factories, prisons, armies, and convents; practices of femininity and masculinity; corporal punishment; fasting, bathing, etiquette, letter writing—the range of studies on various aspects of the body is truly astonishing. But almost without exception, this work, as illuminating as it is, aims at uncovering the social and cultural construction of bodies and only secondarily, if at all, selves. It does not address what is inside the black box of the self, that is, whatever it is in the self that interacts with, limits, and sometimes chooses between different kinds of social construction.[43]

In short, the "iron curtain" between historians and psychology that Harvard historian William L. Langer lamented in 1957 remains standing. Neither psychoanalysis nor academic psychology has yet been able to tear it down. Widespread philosophical, clinical, and cultural criticism of Freud's views; disputes among Freudians themselves over the correct interpretation of Freud's work; the rapid multiplication of alternative forms of clinical practice; and the current enthusiasm for pharmacological treatments of mental illness all served to undermine in their own ways the legitimacy of psychoanalysis and of all forms of talking therapy.

Yet many of Freud's basic insights remain pertinent. Most neuroscientists hold not only that mental activities are susceptible to scientific analysis but also that most mental processes occur unconsciously. While they do not usually give priority, as Freud did, to sexual motivations (and where they do, they are framed in evolutionary terms), many still maintain that the mind includes a sense of self and agency (Freud's ego) and that the mind also serves to connect an individual to social communities (Freud's superego).[44]

The prospects for dialogue between history and psychology are even bleaker when it comes to academic psychology. Psychoanalysis, in its clinical practice, relies on historical narratives in the form of the stories the patient tells the analyst, whereas research psychologists depend on studies of behavior carried out in the laboratory setting and rarely invoke any form of historical interpretation except when it concerns the history of their own discipline. Moreover, academic psychologists have not agreed on a definition of the self. A leading social psychologist who reviewed some thirty thousand articles on the self published between 1974 and 1993 concluded that "the thousands of journal articles dealing with the self have seemed to make the answer to that fundamental question [What is the self?] more elusive rather than clearer."[45]

Not surprisingly, then, some cognitive scientists have come to view the self as a kind of mirage. Their reasoning converges in unexpected ways with those of postmodernists such as Foucault (the self as optical illusion), Derrida (the self as phantasm), and Lacan (the self as misrecognition). The self, according to the psychologist Michael S. Gazzaniga, for example, is a fiction, the illusion that we are in charge of our lives. In his view, "psychology itself is dead." It has been replaced by neuroscience, cognitive science, and evolutionary biology. Yet even Gazzaniga does not deny that there is at least a "sense of self" that plays an important role in the way we think about and act in our lives. In a recent research review on split-brain patients, he argues, "Although it has been difficult to study the 'self' *per se*, there have been intriguing observations about perceptual and cognitive processing relating to the self." In this study, he and his collaborators concluded that a sense of self "arises out of distributed networks in both [left and right] hemispheres [of the brain]."[46]

Given the uncertainties about selfhood, it might seem that any history of the self is next to impossible, yet in one domain, that of the study of emotions, some historians are establishing useful connections with neuroscientists and psychologists. William Reddy delved into cognitive psychology in order to develop a history of emotions in France for the period 1750–1850. He argued that the eighteenth-century emotive style known as sentimentalism played an important role in bringing about the Terror in the French Revolution because it placed so much emphasis on sincerity and patriotic ardor. The governments that followed reined in sentimentalism and yet paradoxically offered more room for individual expression of emotion because they removed the immediate political significance of feelings. Although Reddy's particular claims have been disputed, he has nonetheless opened up a new territory for historical analysis.[47]

Emotions are a promising object of historical study because they show up in historical documents more readily than any other expression of selves. Anger, disgust, fear, happiness, surprise, and sadness can be traced in many different kinds of documents, ranging from court cases to paintings. Some argue that expressions of these emotions are universally recognizable, but even if they are, different contexts produce different outcomes to those recognitions, making cultural and historical studies essential.[48]

As currently understood in neuroscience, emotions are singularly pivotal. Neurologists Hanna and Antonio Damasio, for example, demonstrated in their studies of neurological damage that the emotions are essential elements in reasoning and decision-making. People who lose the ability to feel specific emotions as a result of strokes, head injuries, or tumors also lose the ability to make certain kinds of rational decisions. Thus reason or rationality is not the categorical opposite of emotion or feeling; reason depends on emotion for its functioning. So influential is this kind of research that some now refer to the area of study as "affective cognition" or "the affective sciences."[49]

While acting as a hinge between body and mind in the individual, emotions also connect individuals with society and culture more generally. Emotions start on the individual level with unconscious bodily reactions and develop through a series of steps into self-conscious feelings. Different communities within society have different ways of regulating the expression of emotion, and societies and cultures also vary in the expression of emotions. One important and often overlooked aspect of power, as Reddy affirms, is the capacity to determine the parameters of emotional expression. When we say, for example, that Louis XIV set the tone at his court, we mean that he controlled the ways his courtiers expressed hostility, envy, or even sadness and happiness. The study of regulation of the expression of emotion invites comparisons, not only among historical periods but also among different cultures, non-Western as well as Western. While such comparisons have sometimes been invidious, as in Elias's portrayal of people in the Middle Ages as more impulsive and prone to violence, the work of historians such as Barbara Rosenwein and Ute Frevert demonstrates that they need not be.[50]

From his and Hanna Damasio's work on emotions, Antonio Damasio has developed a model of the neural basis of the self that is at once biological and historical. The self depends, he argues, on evolutionary features of the human brain developed during the Pleistocene Age (i.e., during the emergence of *Homo sapiens*); mind, conscious mind, and conscious mind capable of producing culture emerged in sequence. The self is a perspective "rooted in a relatively stable, endlessly repeated biological state" that gets its core from the structure and operation of the organism and then develops through slowly evolving autobiographical data. The self therefore depends on the continuous reactivation of memories of the past and memories of plans and projects for the possible future, in other words, a historical or narrative sense. The self is simultaneously stable, because it is biologically rooted in the body and brain, and open to history, because this biological state must be continually reactivated and updated with new autobiographical information. There can be no "extended" consciousness, in Damasio's terms, no consciousness of self, without a sense of history, of memories as objects, and of time as a scale that transcends immediate experience.[51]

Although many elements in Damasio's argument have remained the same over time, others have changed, most notably his insistence in recent work on "*primordial feelings*, which signify the existence of my living body independently of how objects engage it or not." He now considers this crucial: "It is the primitive behind all feelings of emotion and therefore is the basis of all feelings caused by interactions between objects and organism." It is one of four elements that in the aggregate constitute a self "in its simple version." The others are having a standpoint for mind based in the body ("this is my body"), the feeling of ownership of mind ("this is my mind"), and the feeling of agency ("the actions being carried out by my body are commanded by my mind"). The key words are perspective (or standpoint), feelings, and by implication embodiment.[52]

Despite the flood of new findings in neuroscience, consciousness and selfhood have yet to be satisfactorily explained in biochemical terms. To quote the philosopher John R. Searle's title for his long review of Damasio's book *Self Comes to Mind* (2010), "the mystery of consciousness continues." In Searle's view, a scientific account of consciousness will one day emerge, but to date it has encountered intractable obstacles: efforts to establish a neuronal correlate of consciousness have so far failed, and theoretical attempts like Damasio's to explain the appearance of consciousness as an interaction between self and mind fall short because they simply transfer the problem of consciousness to either mind or self and end up assuming that the self is already conscious. For Searle, it is consciousness that explains the self, not the other way around, and no one yet has been able to explain the advent of consciousness.[53]

All is not uncertainty, however. Damasio is onto something, Searle grants, when he emphasizes that "in any account of consciousness we need to explain how our conscious states are experienced, not just as a sequence of isolated qualitative subjective events, but as 'my experiences.' " Having a sense of self as the protagonist in the ongoing experiences of the body is crucial to consciousness and ultimately to a sense of agency and identity. This sense of self emerges from the mind's interpretations of the body's interactions in the world.[54]

In the last twenty years, cognitive science has increasingly embraced an embodied view of the mind, rather than an exclusively computational one. In the computational view, the brain is like a computer sifting through representations generated by and located in the brain. In the embodied view, endorsed more vociferously, perhaps, by philosophers of the mind than by neuroscientists, "cognition is not the representation of a pregiven world by a pregiven mind but it is rather the enactment of a world and a mind on the basis of . . . actions that a being in the world performs." In the embodied view, context, which includes the body as well as the environment in the broadest sense, cannot be reduced to sensory input; the interactions between body and brain and body and environment create the self and then propel its continual updating through interactions between self, brain, body, environment, and experience. Perception and action are intertwined; perception does not precede action.[55]

Philosophers who advocate the embodied view of mind often refer back to the phenomenological philosophy of Maurice Merleau-Ponty, who was himself much influenced by studies of childhood cognition. His *Phenomenology of Perception* (1945) drew attention to the philosophical importance of the embodiment of the self. An individual's perception of the world is not solely caused by the impact of sensations from the external world, he argued; it occurs because the self is able to project a world in which the stimulus makes sense. Cognition in his view depends on developing a body schema (he called it a *schéma corporel*) that locates one's body in the world and facilitates an understanding of other bodies. The embodied self therefore develops its own contribution; it can make sense of external sensations or social conditioning only if it acts in its own right.[56]

To hold to a concept of an embodied self is to give priority to the body's interactions with the world. It follows then that mind and body are not separate. This lack of separation might seem obvious since the brain is located in the body and the mind emerges through brain activity, but the separation of mind and body has nonetheless long been a staple of the history of Western philosophy and of Christian theology. Just what mind is once the dualism of mind and body is given up remains to be seen. Even Antonio Damasio, with his clear focus on the mind, equivocates. He aims to trace the biochemical and physical sources of "the mercurial, fleeting business of the mind," but his very choice of language indicates the difficulty involved: "What we experience as mental states corresponds not just to activity in a discrete brain area but rather to the result of massive recursive signaling involving multiple regions." Yet mind remains useful—perhaps even indispensable—for thinking about thinking, and so Damasio uses the term frequently without ever giving a precise definition of it. Like self, it is not a thing, but rather a process.[57]

Focusing on the embodiment of the self or mind makes it possible to see how the self develops out of originally unconscious bodily processes, even if that development is still the subject of considerable debate. The philosopher Shaun Gallagher relies on experimental studies of newborns, sometimes only a few hours old, to get at the earliest sense of self. Although he follows Merleau-Ponty's argument about the importance of a body schema for cognition, he finds it present at birth rather than requiring several months to develop, as Merleau-Ponty had concluded. Gallagher maintains that newborns must already have a primitive body schema at birth because they are able to imitate the actions of other people. In other words, he believes there is an innate body schema. Humans are born with the capacity to immediately start learning about themselves through bodily processes, and it appears that they already have the elements of a rudimentary sense of self at birth. These studies of newborn cognition, as interpreted by Gallagher (he did not do the experiments), answer some of the objections raised by Searle: self does precede consciousness, as Damasio argues, or perhaps emerges simultaneously with consciousness, and both self and consciousness develop over time. Gallagher's argument about a primitive body schema fits with Damasio's account of a proto-self developing into a core self and finally into self-reflexivity, or what Damasio terms "extended consciousness."[58]

What difference might the embodied self make to historians? The meaning of personhood clearly varies culturally and historically; all times and places do not give equal emphasis, for example, to individual autonomy or to the rights of the individual in relation to the family, community, or state. At the same time, there can be no doubt that the self, defined as a sense of ownership of the body, agency in action, and capacity for reflexivity, is indisputably important to the functioning of any human being. It—even if there is dispute about what precisely "it" is—exists. The self should not be imagined as a homunculus (little man) in the head, however. Embodied selves, not brains, make decisions; see, hear, smell, and taste; and are thoughtless or thoughtful. Identity, agency, and selfhood are processes that emerge and continually change in the course of interactions between the brain, the body, and the world. Agency is not just an abstract philosophical issue, as it has often been portrayed. It follows from biological and social development.[59]

The embodied self is, as might be expected, amenable to social contextualization and explanation. Mirror neurons do not just enable social understanding; their development is also influenced by social interactions. Infants respond more rapidly to being the object of attention when they find themselves in more emotion-laden environments. But the study of the effects of social interaction on neurological development has been relatively underdeveloped in part because it is easier, though hardly uncomplicated, to set up experiments on individual brains and in part because much neuroscience assumes that the important things are happening inside brains.[60]

Historians hardly need to be convinced that important things are happening outside of brains; they need to be convinced that something important is happening inside them. Change cannot be explained without some attention to individual selves. Since the brain is wired to develop a sense of self, the self is always, from the very first moment, bringing something to its interaction with the world. The self is shaped by experience, to be sure, but the self also plays a critical role in constituting experience; there can be no experience without a self to apprehend it. The self plays a critical role in constituting experience by giving an experience a place in the self's ongoing development, that is, by interpreting experience, sometimes consciously, sometimes not. Both agency and historical change depend on this interactive relationship between embodied selves and the social or collective dimensions of life. Indeed, what is society other than overlapping intersubjective or inter-self relationships? Moreover, individual consciousness—though embodied and shaped by social interaction—is still capable of reflection and thereby changing the outcome of an action. It does this not through the expression of free will imagined as a kind of disembodied subjectivity or intentionality, but rather through chains of interaction between self, mind, body, and environment and the self's ongoing interpretation of them.[61]

Society and the self should not be reduced to an either-or proposition; society is made up of selves, and selves are shaped by their social or inter-self relations. To some extent, it is as simple as changing perspective. When we consider the standpoint of the crowd as a social collectivity in the French Revolution, for example, we can see an underlying rationale to the attack on the Bastille fortress in July 1789 or even to the horrific prison massacres of September 1792. The Bastille stood for arbitrary and tyrannical government, and the prisoners of 1792 were suspected of collaborating with enemy armies racing toward Paris. When we consider the perspective of the individuals who made up those crowds, the focus changes. Those who gathered together ended up acting in ways none of them could have foreseen or intended. A social interpretation might recapture the underlying rationale and explain who was most likely to join such a group. An interpretation that concentrates on individuals would highlight the ways in which participating in such a collectivity alters the feelings and decisions made by the individuals involved. It therefore gives more attention, potentially, to the somatic experiences that can develop in the course of forming a temporary assemblage under highly charged conditions.

A shift in perspective does not always lead to complementary findings, but more attention to the experience of individuals in crowds is critical to explaining how crowds turn violent. Some social scientists are trying to construct cognitive science models for crowd behavior. This kind of approach emphasizes the intersection between collective dynamics of motion and individual decision-making based on visual and other somatic cues. The virtue of such models is that they do not render crowd behavior irrational or hysterical but rather show how the interaction between individual and collective patterns can develop in different and not always peaceful directions. The models work because they incorporate individual selves.[62]

With the notion of the embodied self, it is possible to move beyond some of the perennially troublesome philosophical and historical dichotomies. There is no necessary opposition between universalism and difference, biology and history, nature and culture, reason and emotion, a stable self and a decentered one, timeless psychology and chronologically rooted history, or, for that matter, individual agency and social construction. Humans are born with the capacity to develop selves and social relations, but the forms they take differ culturally and historically. Needless to say, however, there is still plenty of room for disagreement about exactly how they interconnect, and historians have an important role to play in uncovering historical differences in the development both of selves and of social relations. They will not play that role, however, unless they enter the conversation and start thinking about the self.

FOUR

NEW PURPOSES,
NEW PARADIGMS

History is always under construction but perhaps never more so than in the twenty-first century. The dominant paradigms of the twentieth century have fallen into disrepair. The cultural theories that undermined them revealed their structural weaknesses without drawing up a blueprint for an alternative. Talk of globalization drew attention to a broader landscape but as yet has not yielded a settled paradigm. Still, the prospects for renovation are exciting. New ways of thinking about society and the self can be combined with elements left from past approaches as well as those held out by globalization. The result will be new paradigms that respond to the evolving purposes of the study of history.

History will continue to serve nation-building and identity politics because nation-states still provide the frame for much of political and social life. At the same time history's purposes are expanding as we increasingly think of ourselves as humans sharing with each other and with other species a common

119

planetary past and future. The distant human past, trends in globalization, and changing human relationships to the environment and to other animals are bound to be of growing interest. More and more historical evidence about these new concerns is coming to light from a host of disciplines ranging from archaeology to studies of human and animal genomes. Recent man-made environmental catastrophes such as nuclear accidents and oil spills inevitably draw attention to common global challenges.

These developments do not necessarily feed into a single channel, however. A global, mega-long-term history is not the only story to be told. Historians have always known that answers to historical questions require careful attention to the scale of analysis. If you want to understand *how* industrialization got started in England, for example, you might very well study a city such as Birmingham, one of the sites of early industrialization, or even an individual such as James Watt, who perfected the steam engine. If you want to understand *why* industrialization first started in England, however, you would choose a different angle of vision, comparing England with other countries, such as France, its chief rival in the eighteenth century. More recently, historians have argued for a comparison between England and China, claiming that the technological superiority of the West was far from given in the eighteenth century and that understanding its eventual emergence requires a wider contrast. The scale of the study depends on the question to be answered.[1]

Given the variety of questions that call for a historical approach, no one paradigm is going to rule the roost. Some scholars have concluded that paradigms themselves are of little value, if not positively pernicious, since they inevitably shortchange the diversity of historical experiences. I believe nonetheless that paradigms are necessary; it is in the nature of humans to ask what it means to be human, where we came from, and where we are going. Do we live in a relentlessly modernizing and globalizing world? Will conflicts between classes become more or less acute? Are peasants disappearing across the globe and giving way to a fundamentally different kind of social organization based on gargantuan cities? Are familiar social identities dissolving and new ones emerging to take their place? These are the kinds of questions raised by the previously dominant paradigms in history (modernization, Marxism, the Annales school, and identity politics), and even though the answers given have been contested, the questions continue to haunt us.

Paradigms are problematic because by their nature they focus on only part of the picture, but they are also necessary, if not simply inevitable. Overarching stories, whether centered on a group, a nation, or the entire world, are crucial to the exercise of political and cultural power, which is why Western social scientists are so good at producing paradigms. It is an aspect of Western political and cultural hegemony to control the paradigms. For those who want to resist the power of a dominant group or nation, it is not enough to reject such stories altogether; an alternative narrative is essential. Thus, for example, the 1776 Declaration of Independence of the British North American colonies began with these words: "When in the Course of human events it becomes necessary for one people to dissolve the political bands which have connected them with another and to assume among the powers of the earth, the separate and equal station to which the Laws of Nature and of Nature's God entitle them, a decent respect to the opinions of mankind requires that they should declare the causes which impel them to the separation." The famous reference in the second paragraph to the self-evident truths "that all men are created equal, that they are endowed by their Creator with certain unalienable Rights" had long-lasting resonance, but it occupied only a small space within the larger narrative of King George III's "repeated injuries and usurpations" aimed at establishing "an absolute Tyranny over these States." Independence depended on developing a narrative that recast the history of the colonies and their place in the wider world. Narratives, whether at the level of ethnic identity, national unity, the history of the West, or the history of the world, are crucial for establishing a sense of place in a wider order and for changing that order itself.[2]

Storytelling is an essential feature of human development. Narrative organizes individual memory, the sense of self, and even the individual notion of reality. Certain brain injuries, depending on the region affected, correlate with different kinds of "dysnarrativia," which can take the form of arrested narration (amnesia), unbounded narration (fabricated narratives with little or no relationship to actual events), undernarration (inability to choose between different narrative outcomes that follow from prospective choices), and denarration (inability to invest narrative scenarios with affect). As one recent handbook of child psychology affirms, "Narrative is a cultural universal, one of the most powerful interpretive tools that human beings possess for organizing experience in time and interpreting and valuing human action."[3]

The ability to narrate is a universal human trait on a cultural as well as an individual level. Roland Barthes insisted that "narrative is present in every age, in every place, in every society; it begins with the very history of mankind and there nowhere is nor has been a people without narrative. . . . Caring nothing for the division between good and bad literature, narrative is international, transhistorical, transcultural: it is simply there, like life itself." Moreover, all cultures have overarching stories or meta-narratives, whether they call them that or not, because all cultures have stories about their origins, about what matters in life, and about how they have come to occupy their place in the world.[4]

Clifford Geertz recounts a marvelous story about such meta-narratives toward the beginning of his *Interpretation of Cultures*. An Englishman, having been told by his Indian interlocutor that the world rested on a platform which rested on the back of an elephant, which in turn rested on the back of a turtle, then asked what the turtle rested on. The answer was another turtle, and other turtles all the way down. Geertz interpreted this account as a metaphor for the work of anthropology and concluded that it was impossible to get to the bottom of anything, that "cultural analysis is intrinsically incomplete." He then went on to make the case for "thick description" as opposed to causal explanation as the best way of making sense of a culture. "Culture," he said, is the "webs of significance" spun by man, and the analysis of it should be "not an experimental science in search of law but an interpretive one in search of meaning."[5]

Geertz's opposition between science, law, and cause on one side and culture, interpretation, and meaning on the other is too stark. The story shows, after all, that everyone wants a causal explanation of the origins of the world even if all such causal explanations eventually run into a wall. To seek the origins of the world, the story confirms, is to pursue an infinite regression: it is to ask what came before the beginning of time. So the Indian's response reveals a universal predicament and a universal difficulty, but it also demonstrates the inevitability of causal thinking. We all construct narratives that explain our individual and collective places in the world, and we all therefore engage in causal thinking. Jean Piaget thought that children developed causal understanding around age seven or eight, but more recent research has shown that children as young as two years old understand causal relations between events and states of mind and have the ability to express those relations in language. Causal reasoning is universal.[6]

Geertz's tale suggests yet another message, this one about Western feelings of superiority that are related to the difficulty of explaining the origins of the world. The Englishman was apparently left speechless by the Indian's account. How exactly might he have proved it wrong? We can imagine that the Englishman nonetheless felt a certain smugness about the Indian's inability to come up with a truly final cause like that of the Christian God. For believers, God's existence by definition requires no cause: the Christian God, as it were, is the mother of all turtles.

Historians usually do not bother much about the origins of the world, unless they write truly planetary histories, but they do have to wrestle with the question of history's meaning. Does history have an implicit goal, whether that goal is defined as freedom, progress, modernity, or globalization? In one of the most influential formulations, the early-nineteenth-century German philosopher G. W. F. Hegel claimed that "the history of the world is none other than the progress of the consciousness of Freedom." That progress implied a linear historical development: "The East knew and to the present day knows only that *One* is free; the Greek and Roman world that *some* are free; the German world knows that *All* are free." The present is therefore superior to the past, and the West is superior to the East in Hegel's view.[7]

This kind of teleological thinking is not easy to overcome and is to some extent implicit in the very idea of a paradigm with its overarching story. Stories by definition have beginnings and ends, and it is very difficult not to read the end of the story back into the past. Narrative itself is hard to separate from ends or goals since it is always constructed from a moment that is inherently retrospective. A narrative explains how the past led to the present, or how events further in the past led to outcomes not as far in the past, so the present inevitably serves as a goal of the narrative. The philosopher David Carr argues that narrative is teleological because all human action is teleological; action derives its meaning from its projected end and the narrative reflects this goal.[8]

Darwin supposedly ended the teleological thinking that provided the foundation for biology up to his time, but even his principle of natural selection lends itself to teleological thinking when viewed in retrospect; the organisms that survived were those that adapted best to their environment. Thus evolution seems to reveal a pattern and purpose over the long run. Even hard-core materialists such as Marx, who rejected religion and anything resembling Aristotelian metaphysics, nonetheless wanted to believe that history itself revealed an underlying purpose, which for Marx was the final elimination of class struggle through the victory of the proletariat in a communist revolution. Can looking back in time be other than teleological?

The key element in creating this conundrum is the point of view of the narrator. If one writes, as Hegel did, to explain the superiority of the West, then the superiority of the West becomes the telos of the story. If one looks at organisms after natural selection has taken place, then those who survive are the fittest. Narrating the self, one asks, "How did I get here, to this moment in time?" Everything then seems to lead, despite all obstacles and detours, to the end point.

The solution, for historians, is not to refuse narrative altogether, as some tried to suggest in the post–World War II decades. Historians who hoped to bring history closer to the natural or at least closer to the social sciences argued that historians should stick to analysis and steer away from narrative; like scientists, historians would systematically accumulate quantifiable evidence to test hypotheses with the hope of establishing causal explanations. The Annales-school historian Emmanuel Le Roy Ladurie famously maintained that "the only scientific history is quantifiable history." The quantifiers bought into the same dichotomy declared by Geertz between science and cultural interpretation, but chose the former.[9]

This attempt at a more scientific approach fell short for many reasons, but the most important was the impossibility of separating analysis and causal explanation from narrative. In fact, every causal explanation implies a narrative and every narrative implies causal explanation. In a study of the way people understand narrative texts, the experimental psychologists Arthur C. Graesser, Murray Singer, and Tom Trabasso concluded that making sense of narratives rested on three elements: the reader's goals, the need for coherence, and the development of plausible explanations for actions and events. In short, a narrative cannot be understood unless the reader is able to envisage causal explanations, however implicit or naive. Moreover, narrative comprehension, because it depends on the reader's goals and the impulse to find coherence, necessarily has a teleological element. The philosopher Paul Ricoeur argues in *Time and Narrative* that "causal and teleological argument—irreducible to each other, and compatible—fuse in the meaning we attach to an action." In other words, humans look for a logic in their stories that is related to their own goals.[10]

Historians therefore can hardly eliminate teleology altogether, though they can get some purchase on the tendency to impose grandiose end points like freedom and modernization. While it is legitimate and even necessary to attempt to write the history of the world, as Hegel tried to do, his example demonstrates the dangers of taking one's own time as the goal of history. The overarching story of freedom, systemized by Hegel, had taken shape toward the end of the eighteenth century; that of progress, in the nineteenth (Hegel combined them in one way, Marx in another); modernization, in the twentieth (in response to the perceived failures of Marxism); and globalization, in the twenty-first century (in response to the perceived failures of both modernization and Marxism). Thus all the major narratives are responses to particular moments in time, and while they have proved fruitful in some regards, they have also served to block understanding in other ways. We may not be able to give them up, but we can at least recognize their limitations.

A first step, then, is to recognize that history as it unfolds has no set course, even if our attempts to narrate it slip such teleological elements back in. There is no pre-given goal or intelligent design determining the outcome of history. Yet history is not directionless, and trends can be deciphered, including greater density of planetary population and increasing social interaction and differentiation of social functions. Once density, interaction, and differentiation reached a certain level, then resources became available for specialized forms of knowledge and for technological development. With increasing social interaction, specialized knowledge, and technological development, individuals and societies developed a sharper consciousness of time and its passage, leading to a sense of the acceleration of time. But these processes should not be thought of as arrows flying straight to their targets. There are no targets. Cultures appear and disappear, social interaction and differentiation can stop or speed up, hegemony over territory varies in its duration and has never been permanent, and technological development is never uniform, much less uniformly positive, in its outcomes. All kinds of unexpected consequences can attend the movement of the various arrows.[11]

Since history has no preordained end point, modernity must be considered a problematic notion. To be sure, fundamental, transformational changes have occurred in the last three centuries. In the West and increasingly elsewhere, people experienced themselves as more and more separate from their communities and even to some extent their families. Society was imagined as a zone of freedom from transcendental forms of authority. Social functions became so dramatically differentiated and technological development so rapid that they drew insistent commentary. But these changes did not occur all at once or everywhere in the same manner.

Modernity has served too often as the telos of history rather than as a handy phrase for a set of interconnected, ongoing developments. Modernity does not represent a rupture in history, dividing into separate realms the premodern or traditional on one side of the line and the modern on the other. Many characteristics of what is supposed to be modernity developed over several centuries and at varying rhythms in different places. The use of "modernity" has led to lazy history, in which it becomes easy to overlook, misunderstand, or denigrate everything that fails to foster the traits associated with modernity.

If globalization is to develop into a convincing paradigm, then it must avoid putting forward modernity as the inevitable end point. Globalization need not be so closely tied to modernization. It precedes modernization and as a process has had different causes over time, ranging from climate change (early humans, some theorize, left Africa during an Ice Age heat wave) to religion (the spread of Christianity, Islam, or Buddhism), conquest, and commerce. Historians are playing a vital role in the refinement of theories of globalization by showing how the process worked at various moments in time. Rather than start from the present and look backward, they start at a point in the past and ask how different alternatives sorted themselves out going forward. In this way, they effectively sidestep the teleological trap.

Historians are also casting doubt on the supposedly close connection between globalization and capitalism. Earlier forms of globalization clearly had other sources, and even when the trade in goods is the focus, scholars often end up showing the importance of social and cultural factors in driving economic expansion. In a wide-ranging essay on the limits of globalization in the early modern world, for example, economic historian Jan de Vries offers an overview of intercontinental trade between Europe and Asia. He documents a 25-fold increase in that trade between 1500 and 1800. Although Europeans imported goods from their New World colonies during the same period that were valued three times higher, Asian imports had an impact beyond their monetary value. Asian imports of spices, tea, silk, and porcelain stimulated, in de Vries's terms, "new European consumer wants." In response, Europeans frequently figured out new ways to supply those demands from other places, with Caribbean coffee and sugar, for instance, and European-made porcelains and textiles. The story is not just one of globalizing commerce, therefore, or of simple European dominance. It is a story about what economists call "elasticity of demand."[12]

When economists talk about elasticity of demand, they usually mean price elasticity, that is, how much demand for goods fluctuates in relationship to its price. But consumer wants are not just about relative supply and demand or prices, especially when new products are at issue. Sometimes consumer demand arises from newly discovered expectations. Tobacco, for example, was introduced to the French in the sixteenth century by the French ambassador to Lisbon, Jean Nicot (whence the term "nicotine"), who planted a specimen brought from

Florida in his garden in Portugal. Having heard reports of its medicinal uses by natives in the New World, Nicot verified these properties for himself by treating various members of his household for ulcers, wounds, and ringworm. He then sent it to the French king to treat two of the ladies at court who had carcinomas. Although consumers moved on to more recreational uses for tobacco, it continued to be prescribed until the middle of the nineteenth century for an astonishing variety of ailments, from nasal polyps to insect bites. It was even administered by rectum to halt hemorrhoidal bleeding. The demand for tobacco grew at first because consumers thought it would work as a medicine.[13]

Consumer demand can be explained only by paying attention to changing cultural contexts and the way they are shaped by individual wishes. In a marvelous analysis of the explosion of the demand for rhubarb in the early modern period, Erika Monahan recounts how a pud (thirty-six pounds) of Chinese rhubarb in Siberia cost three times more than a house, a horse, or a slave in the seventeenth century. It was worth five times more than that in Moscow and even more in Western Europe. She cites a combination of factors for its increased value in the seventeenth century: European conquests led to the discovery of previously unknown plants, like tobacco, that natives were using as medicines; the rising prestige and popularization of sciences such as botany made elites in particular more attentive to these discoveries and to the prospect of finding curative qualities in plants closer to home, like rhubarb; increased travel brought European doctors into contact with Chinese rhubarb, which turned out to be more potent than European varieties, making it more desirable as a purgative; and purgatives were especially valued because Western (and Islamic) medicine had for centuries placed great emphasis on cleansing, for example, purging or bloodletting, because physicians believed illness was caused by an imbalance in vital fluids called humors. Finally, the spread of print disseminated knowledge of new or preferred remedies more widely, and more discretionary income made it possible for ordinary people to seek these remedies from their local apothecaries. As Monahan shows, no one factor, and certainly not just its relative scarcity, explains the profitability of Chinese rhubarb.[14]

Monahan's study exemplifies the contribution that historians can make to globalization theories. It is a powerful example of following a historical topic forward rather than tracing it backward. Like tobacco and tomatoes, rhubarb was one of the plants Columbus stumbled upon in the New World. It had an indisputable role in early modern globalization. Unlike tobacco and tomatoes, however, it gradually lost its global importance as medical understanding changed and new purgatives were created in the laboratory. Still, its successes and its longer-term failures—unlike tobacco and corn, it could not be grown on large-scale plots of land—tell us much about the globalization process at a specific moment in time.

Our understanding of how rhubarb contributed to globalization would be even better if we knew more about how individuals felt about buying and taking rhubarb, about the need to cleanse their bodies, about having more discretionary income, and therefore about having more choices available to them. In short, we need to learn more about what was in the minds of people living between 1500 and 1800. This information is not easy to find, but historians attentive to emotions are beginning to uncover more of it. Consumers wanted rhubarb because it helped them regulate their bodily excretions. People in early modern Europe thought of their bodies not in terms of individual organs but as the site of constant alterations in heat, cold, and emotions that required bleeding, cupping, vomiting, and purging to restore its fragile equilibrium.[15]

Bodily excretions were filled with medical, emotional, and even legal significance. Physicians closely examined the color of urine, the quality of spittle and stools, and the amount of sweat. Since doctors and patients alike believed that health depended on a balance of the four humors—black bile, yellow (or red) bile, blood, and phlegm—the physical appearance of excretions was a crucial indicator. A balance of emotions was considered essential to good health, but balance did not just mean moderation; it also meant an ability to express emotions in appropriate social settings. Emotions had to flow from one individual to another just as bodily fluids had to circulate in the right manner. Too great a grief was bad for health, but too little was a signal of even more serious problems. The female victims of the witchcraft persecutions that swept Europe from the mid-sixteenth to the end of the seventeenth century were often described as "dry" and cold women because they did not cry at their trials. Tears could have legal standing.[16]

Rhubarb, then, brings us back to the self-society intersection. Globalization depends on growing demand, which can be explained only by paying attention to changes in both societies and selves. The study of self-society interactions is a vast and still largely virgin territory for historians, but investigation of these interactions promises great yields. In the rest of this chapter, I outline one set of such changes in the eighteenth-century West: the transition from an embodied self oriented toward equilibrium in bodily fluids and emotions to an embodied self looking for increased stimulation and participation in shared spaces, including politics.

The evidence for this shift can be found in many places but has not been brought together in one place because scholars have directed their attention elsewhere: to the economic aspects of new products rather than their meanings for buyers; to the nation-state dimensions of democratization rather than its meanings for individuals; to how society controls selves rather than to how selves push against social constraints; to laws and intellectual conceptions of individualism rather than to emotions and bodily expressions of a sense of self. The shift from a self oriented toward equilibrium to one inclined toward stimulation is not a conscious evolution explicated by physicians, philosophers, or politicians. Evidence for it must be sought in a combination of direct and indirect sources ranging from personal letters and commentaries on new products and practices to paintings and engravings of ordinary people. Here only the tiniest bit of the terrain can be turned over in the hope of showing, nonetheless, that this change in the experience of the self had momentous economic, social, and political consequences.[17]

Tobacco, coffee, and tea were essential ingredients in the transformation. Like tobacco, coffee and tea were first prized for their medicinal uses. As their consumption spread from the upper to the lower classes in the late seventeenth and the eighteenth century, they took on meanings having more to do with their pleasurable qualities. In 1675 the French aristocrat Marie de Sévigné compared her favorite perfume to tobacco:

"It is a folly like tobacco; when you get used to it, you cannot live without it." In her letters she also constantly commented on coffee, recounting her efforts to give it up but always coming back to it in the end. A century later, in the 1780s, French writer Louis-Sébastien Mercier remarked on the drift of coffee drinking down the social scale: "Coffee drinking has become a habit, and one so deep-rooted that the working classes will start the day on nothing else." English and Dutch painters and engravers often depicted coffeehouses, whereas French painters gloried in the portrayal of women being served coffee, sometimes by black servants or slaves. For French artists such as Carle van Loo and Nicolas Lancret, coffee, women, and pleasure went together.[18]

These once exotic products served as relay points connecting newly felt individual desires with social patterns that arose in response. Ordinary people discovered a taste for tobacco, coffee, and tea, a taste now linked to stimulation and pleasure rather than to cures for ailments. But once upper-class people saw the lower classes indulging in what had once been more elite activities, they began to insist on their social distinction in new ways. In the eighteenth century, snuff came into fashion so that the upper classes could separate themselves from the pipe-smoking lower classes and Native Americans. Prosperous people patronized coffeehouses while workers in cities like Paris took their coffee with milk and sugar from female street vendors. Tea, on the other hand, was associated primarily with women and with domestic consumption, though in England male workers also gulped it down.[19]

The desiring, deciding, stimulus-seeking self developed in tandem with an increasing social awareness. Snuff taking, for example, fostered social distinction, but it also encouraged a greater sense of individualism as snuff takers had to choose between a wide variety of scents and preparations and a glittering array of snuffboxes while following the latest fashions in sniffing or inhaling the powder. Coffee drinking also promoted both individual choice and new forms of socializing. Marie de Sévigné advised her adored daughter to take Narbonne honey in her coffee rather than sugar. Choice was especially at issue, however, when it came to frequenting particular coffeehouses. Artists and writers such as William Hogarth and Henry Fielding went to Old Slaughter's coffeehouse in St. Martin's Lane, London. Some chose their coffeehouse based on their politics—the Cocoa-tree Club for Tories and St. James for Whigs in London—and still others went to the coffeehouse that carried the papers they wanted to read. As new social practices spread, the opportunities for individual choices multiplied.

Teahouses never caught on in Western Europe the way they did in Asia and even Russia, though a certain number of public tea gardens did attract a middle-class English clientele in the summer. As imports of tea began to increase in the early seventeenth century, the beverage stimulated a cascading series of consumption demands, especially in the Anglophone world, where drinking tea took root in the middle and upper classes as a domestic activity. Taking tea became a new leisure time activity for women and began to be identified with politeness, since afternoon tea often included men. Tea from China soon brought in its wake Chinese porcelain teapots, dishes to hold the teapots, spoon boats, not to mention cups and saucers. Among those trying to capitalize on this demand for Chinese porcelain, available only to the very prosperous, was the English pottery-maker Josiah Wedgwood. In 1765 he filled an order for British Queen Charlotte, who requested a complete set of "tea things" in Wedgwood's cream ware, a ceramic he had developed for its creamy color. Wedgwood quickly marketed this as "Queen's ware" to aristocrats and royalty around Europe and then used his reputation to sell dinner services to middling sorts at home. More and more people bought "China," expressing both individual desires and social aspirations.

The changes that followed from tea drinking in the Anglophone world were astounding when considered over the long term. Under the influence of tea, all meals gradually became important domestic activities. Eating became both more social and more individual. Rather than gulping down one's food in a hurry off a knife or fork or fingers, people now sat down at a table and ate off individual plates. Women no longer stood to serve but joined other members of the household at the table. Eating or drinking tea together signaled civilization and refinement, as did the equal partaking of women in these activities.[20]

New print forms such as newspapers, magazines, and novels benefited from, if they did not in fact grow out of, the taste for tea and coffee, and their publics included women too. In 1711, the new daily *The Spectator* opined, "I shall be ambitious to have it said of me, that I have brought Philosophy out of Closets and Libraries, Schools and Colleges, to dwell in Clubs and Assemblies, at Tea-tables and in Coffee-houses." The editor Joseph Addison hoped specifically to "recommend these my Speculations to all well-regulated Families, that set apart an Hour in every Morning for Tea and Bread and Butter; and would earnestly advise them for their Good to order this Paper to be punctually served up, and to be looked upon as a Part of the Tea Equipage." The new dailies were being sold as accessories to the newly popular beverage.[21]

Consumption democratized in the eighteenth century and in turn promoted the democratization of politics. A study of probate inventories for Annapolis, Maryland, shows that tea tables first appeared in estates of the wealthy in the 1720s and then made their way into the belongings of the middle classes in the 1740s and the poor thereafter. Cups and saucers followed a similar trajectory. The popularity of tea in the American colonies made it a singularly effective rallying point for resistance to British authority. Although the upper classes still desired to maintain their social distinction, it is clear that they had reason to worry about the maintenance of hierarchy.[22]

The democratization of politics followed, but not because ordinary people now had access to more items for consumption. It followed because ordinary people learned through consuming that their choices mattered, even if many of them were making the same choices. People took tobacco, coffee, and tea for many reasons, but high on the list was stimulation. Workers in particular consumed immense quantities of coffee and tea. Mercier remarked on Parisian workers claiming that if they had coffee for breakfast they could keep going all day even if they ate nothing else. In England heavily sweetened tea often took the place of a meal for working people. Sugar consumption in England went from four to eighteen pounds a person over the course of the eighteenth century.[23]

The democratization of politics followed from the mutually reinforcing expansion of selves and societies in the eighteenth century. If the stimulus-seeking self gradually edged out the self oriented toward equilibrium, it did so across webs of self-society interactions. Marie de Sévigné once again provides a telling example because she lived on the cusp of the change. She tried to navigate between coffee's effects on the body's equilibrium and the recurring desire—hers, her daughters, and her friends—for coffee. In November 1679 she insisted to her daughter that coffee heats and agitates the blood and was therefore bad for her beloved daughter's fragile health. Yet in April 1694 she wrote to her daughter that coffee "will console me for everything [she was preparing for a purge]" and "bring me closer to you." The two versions of the self were in tension with each other for Sévigné.[24]

Coffeehouses provided a different kind of self-society interaction, and because they were public spaces, coffeehouses had direct political consequences. Ironically, even while the British were making tea at home into a drink associated with their national identity, coffeehouses also flourished in England, Scotland, and Ireland and brought together coffee, conviviality, newspapers, and politics. Coffeehouses spread from England in the 1650s to Ireland in the 1660s and Scotland in the 1670s. Women sometimes frequented them and on occasion became proprietors of their own coffeehouses. Coffeehouses became synonymous with a newly demanding public, whose impact then expanded across Western Europe. The first cafés appeared in Paris in the 1670s, in Vienna in the 1680s, and in Berlin in the 1720s.[25]

Coffeehouses hosted discussions of science or literature but above all else political talk. They carried the pamphlets, satirical broadsheets, and newspapers of the moment. Coffee-houses so evidently set the temperature of political discussion that governments across Europe sent their undercover agents to report on what was being said in them. King Charles II of Britain tried to suppress them in 1675, and his advisors wanted to limit the circulation of news as well, without success. In the early eighteenth century, the police reported to King Louis XIV of France that while popular cabarets posed no threat, "in cafés, politics is discussed by malcontents who speak wrongly of affairs of state." Louis's successors had even more to fear from cafés. The leading figures of the eighteenth-century Enlightenment, including Voltaire, Rousseau, and Diderot, met friends, discussed philosophy, and played chess in their favorite cafés. On July 12, 1789, the young journalist Camille Desmoulins jumped onto a café table in the Palais Royal in Paris and exhorted his listeners to take up arms to defend free-dom. In this way, it might be said that coffee led eventually to revolution.[26]

It did so, however, through a series of intermediate steps. Tobacco, coffee, and tea became widely available in the eigh-teenth century. Coffee consumption, for example, increased 200-fold in Europe between 1700 and 1800, largely thanks to the extension of coffee cultivation, first to the Dutch col-onies of Java and Surinam and then to French colonies in the Caribbean. Why did people develop a taste for these products? Increasing European contacts with the New World, the Middle East, and Asia certainly played a part, as did the proliferation of books and pamphlets recounting those adventures. Yet new consumption patterns did not follow inevitably. Prices had to go down because of increased supply, but supply would not have increased if consumers had not developed a taste for the new products. They did so because people increasingly opted for stimulation, novelty, individual choice, and meeting together in spaces outside the market, the church, and the family. Tastes changed as the experience of the self changed, and as tastes and selves changed, so did social prospects. It may be impossible to say which came first, new selves or new social outlooks, but both had to occur. People learned to make new kinds of choices, and at the same time, the texture of society became more varied, affording more arenas for individual choices.[27]

In short, the domain of the self and the domain of society expanded together. New kinds of energy were tapped in the emotionally charged spaces of interpersonal interaction. Unlike Foucault, who locates the source of all productive energy in power, usually as expressed in institutions and their practices, I find it in the spaces in which each individual mind engages with other minds and in the process creates the collective, intersubjective domain of practices and understandings known as society. The social conventions that shape the expectations or behaviors of individuals operate in these interpersonal spaces, but so too do the individual minds that interpret, incorporate, sometimes resist, and sometimes simply choose between social conventions. As the domains of the self and society expanded, so too did the prospect of new expectations and behaviors such as drinking coffee, sitting in coffeehouses, and grumbling about the ruler's politics. Revolution grew out of the interaction between increasingly autonomous, deciding, stimulus-seeking selves and an increasingly autonomous, demanding society.[28]

Emotional energy is not fixed, like some kind of universal

constant. It has increased dramatically in the Western world over the last few centuries as the domain of the self and the domain of society have expanded together, mutually reinforcing each other even at points of tension and conflict. Democratic or representative politics are one important consequence of this growth of energy, and at the same time, a booster for its continuing increase. Democracy became imaginable only when large numbers of individuals could make claims to their rights and when societies could claim rights against their monarchical and aristocratic rulers, that is, when selves and societies extended the range of their claims in tandem. The rights of individuals to autonomy and political participation and the assertion of a social contract underlying all government developed in interaction with each other from the sixteenth century onward.

The story of the rise of democratic forms of political participation has been told countless times, but missing from those accounts is any attention to the emotions that generated the process and increased in response. To stake a claim to rights, whether on the part of the individual or on the part of society, was to demand a new space for action and new meanings for the activities that would take place there. These actions and meanings in turn created enhanced status for individuals and societies. Since a claim to one kind of right (e.g., political participation for "all men") almost invariably engendered other claims (e.g., political rights of those without property, of religious minorities, and of women), the process worked as a kind of spiral pulling in more people and generating more energy.

Evidence for the emergence of this democratic spiral might be found from the sixteenth century forward (and probably much further back too), but the French Revolution provides a particularly striking example because the energies created then vividly impressed many observers. Needless to say, it is impossible to measure interpersonal or social energy with some kind of meter, but those who witnessed events in 1789 saw something exceptional transpiring. The Anglo-Irish politician Edmund Burke was among the most perspicacious and enduring in influence as he gave voice to an emergent and reactive conservatism. In 1790 he pronounced, "All circumstances taken together, the French Revolution is the most astonishing that has hitherto happened in the world. . . . Everything seems out of nature in this strange chaos of levity and ferocity."[29] He sensed that the explosion of new energies would transform entire ways of life.

Burke focused his attention in particular on the women's march to Versailles in October 1789. The October Days, as they were called, had begun as a typical eighteenth-century food riot by women complaining about the price of bread. It quickly turned into something more far-reaching. Men joined in, and they all marched to the center of national power just outside of Paris. Burke describes the events, and especially the procession returning the king and queen to Paris, in lurid terms: "The royal captives who followed in the train were slowly moved along, amidst the horrid yells, and shrilling screams, and frantic dances, and infamous contumelies, and all the unutterable abominations of the furies of hell, in the abused shape of the vilest of women." Yet even Burke knew that these supposedly atavistic scenes of female frenzy portended an entirely new world in which calculation would displace chivalry, kings and queens would be considered no different from ordinary people, and what he notoriously termed "the swinish multitude" would become the source of governmental legitimacy.[30]

In the whirlwind that continued to gather force, the monarch and the assembly, and ultimately the monarchy itself, had to bow before the people's embodied will. The deeds of those days—actions of embodied selves now seeking a greater say in public affairs—changed the nature of power relations within the government and opened the way to even more radical changes in social relations. The heightened levels of fear and exhilaration that ensued touched millions of individual bodies and helped stimulate the proliferation of pamphlets, newspapers, songs, cartoons, and broadsheets. New energies fueled political discussion and emerging forums of political mobilization such as clubs. Political newspapers, clubs, caucuses within the legislature, and electoral agitation at the local level all fed off these energies and at the same time worked to channel, and yes, even to discipline, them. A different political order emerged as individuals acting together erased the previous map of power.

While Burke experienced horror, many of his contemporaries felt positively electrified. The English poet Robert Southey described his reaction in a letter to a friend: "what a visionary world seemed to open upon [us] . . . nothing was dreamt of but the regeneration of the human race." The "orgasm of the Revolution," as Southey described it to Samuel Taylor Coleridge, was certainly a striking bodily metaphor, though just what Southey meant by it is not certain. Poets, religious and political radicals, and even scientists in England in this period deliberately set about experimenting with their personal relationships, with the idea of democracy, and in some cases with both hallucinogenic gases and poetic styles. At times, they ran into personal and political trouble, but they delighted in thinking of themselves as explorers of the depths of emotions and of the heights of new political forms.[31]

When the scientist Humphry Davy isolated nitrous oxide in his laboratory, for example, he did not use it at first as the painkiller it became. He and his friends, among them Southey, Coleridge, Tom Wedgwood of the porcelain family, and Gregory Watt, the youngest son of the inventor of the steam engine, tried it out as a drug that enhanced sensations. Davy wrote in his laboratory notebook that it gave him "a thrilling in the chest and extremities[,] highly pleasurable impressions were perceived at the same time with vivid ideas, hearing was more acute; & general pleasurable feeling seemed to absorb existence."[32] The stimulus-seeking self was clearly at work.

Although most of these same young men, like their mutual friend William Wordsworth, eventually repented of their early democratic enthusiasms, their experiences also had longer-lasting effects, now generally known under the rubric of romanticism. They linked personal exploration inside a circle of like-minded friends with the new style of poetry. Watt wrote to his friend Davy in 1801 about the effect of reading true poetry: "The magical letters embrace him more closely and he unconsciously exists in a circle of enchantment—his senses are gradually bewildered in a delightful maze[;] unable to retreat he eagerly advances deeper and deeper till he is only delivered from his fascinating entanglement by—the end of the performance and he is left with the indistinct recollections of pleasure."[33]

These various experiences and events had somatic impacts that translated into new thoughts and conceptions of the individual, society, and politics. The possibilities of democratic participation, the search for depths of the self, and romantic poetry's emphasis on heightened individual experience all had antecedents in previous discourses and disciplinary practices. But these discourses and practices cannot fully explain them. Experiences and events sometimes burst the confines of the expected. That is how individuals grow, societies change, and new political orders develop.

The French Revolution cannot be analyzed in Foucaultian terms as power producing new disciplinary strategies that in turn mobilize new kinds of social behavior. During the cascading events of the French Revolution, the sequence is reversed: new kinds of individual and social behavior created the conditions for new strategies of power and discipline. In the chemical chain reaction that constitutes a momentous event, the interaction between individuals takes on forms previously unimagined. The French Revolution always lurks beneath the surface of Foucault's own accounts, since he traced many new disciplinary strategies to the end of the eighteenth and beginning of the nineteenth century. But he never gives it a positive role. In this, Foucault followed the example of his intellectual guide, Friedrich Nietzsche, who viewed the French Revolution as the triumph of all that was most slavish in modern life, the herd mentality that he associated with democratic politics. In contrast, I view the French Revolution as an example of how the energies of ordinary people can catalyze and in turn be transformed by extraordinary events.[34]

The synergistic growth of self and society necessarily

involves a constant tug of war between freedom and discipline. Foucault gave all his attention to discipline and considered freedom merely a kind of by-product. Prison could function only as an institution, after all, if freedom had some fundamental value that could be taken away. Foucault showed little interest in this tension, preferring to concentrate on how discipline functioned. Yet even the prison was a product of this ever-expanding emotional energy animating self and society.

Some form of incarceration has probably always existed, if only to hold those awaiting trial and punishment, but imprisonment took on new forms from the sixteenth century onward. At that time, local governments in England, the Netherlands, and some northern German towns began to consign vagrants, beggars, debtors, and other troublesome individuals to workhouses. These new attempts at disciplining unruly individuals would never have come about if unruliness were not perceived to be a growing problem. Families also used such institutions to put away members who threatened family honor, but behind such decisions we can also see individuals increasingly testing the limits of family control, that is, increasing demands for personal autonomy.[35]

Incarceration, however, rarely served as a punishment for crime, which well into the eighteenth century took corporal forms: placement in the pillory, whipping, branding, forced labor in the galleys, or transportation to overseas colonies, not to mention breaking the body on the wheel for capital offenses. Most of these declined in use as eighteenth-century authorities turned away from public spectacles of inflicting bodily pain. The prison as punishment took their place. Foucault sees in this development the emergence of an even more sinister form of power in which surveillance, classification, and enforcement of routines are used to control and reshape individuals. Reformers at the time thought they were introducing more rational and humane methods of punishment that showed concern for individuals.[36]

The story now appears to be more paradoxical than either of these positions would suggest, and the paradox was created by tensions between the self and society. On the one hand, public opinion turned against the state's use of brutal corporal punishments that were increasingly seen as violating the individual's bodily dignity. The sacredness once tied to the church, as custodian of the body and blood of Jesus, and to the king's body alone among those in secular society, was dispersed to all bodies, which were considered equally sacred and inviolable. Justice could not include violation of individual selves. On the other hand, because crime was now considered an attack on individuals rather than on the community, it could not be expiated by a community ceremony. Local authorities and families gradually lost the privilege of shutting away the unruly while governments turned toward locking up criminals rather than marking their bodies or sending them away to the galleys and forced labor.[37]

If individuals were now sacred, why were some of them excluded from society, whether in prisons or mental asylums? Prisons removed criminals from society in order to rehabilitate them for reintegration into society, or at least so the theory went. Prisons offered a very different solution from branding, which marked someone as different forever, or from transportation to the colonies, which quite literally removed convicts from the home society. Similarly, asylums can be seen as a means for integrating the mad into society through treatment rather than as tools for their complete exclusion, as Foucault argued. Underlying the effort at inclusion is a notion not just of the sacredness of the person but also of radical sameness. Prisons and asylums grew out of the conviction that criminals and insane people were like everyone else. They were signs of the new democratic inclusiveness, never fully achieved needless to say, but signs of it nonetheless.[38]

Thus as both self and society expanded their domains, every time a push was made for individual freedoms—from bodily violation, in the case of criminal punishment—discipline pulled in a different direction—toward prison as an institution, in this case. Yet discipline always came up against limits as individual inmates thwarted, evaded, or even forcibly resisted the restrictions placed upon their freedom to act. In the ultimate irony, solitary confinement, which was made feasible by the reformist zeal to house prisoners in well-aerated individual cells rather than fetid mass holding-pens, became the cruelest of disciplinary practices. There is no space for freedom, even the tiniest, most regulated freedom, unless there is communication between individuals. Freedom becomes meaningful only if other people are involved.

The general increase in emotional energy over the last few centuries cannot be attributed to the expansion of capitalism. The capitalist system generally thrives on subservient workers, not workers primed to make demands for better working conditions and universal suffrage. It seems more likely that the expanding domains of self and society helped fuel the spread of capitalism; people aspiring for more personal freedom were more likely to move to towns and cities and consider new kinds of jobs. In any case, tautology always seems to creep into arguments about capitalism or modernization; whatever happens turns out to be just what capitalism needed at that very moment.

I prefer an explanation that combines psychological and social, intra-European and global factors and that privileges no single one of them. In the sixteenth century, the Protestant Reformation opened new spaces for individual conscience and decision-making, and at the same time, it insisted on new forms of personal discipline, such as Bible reading and religious worship within the family. Once the power of these new arrangements became apparent, some of them were also embraced, albeit with important modifications, by Catholicism. At the same time, European voyages across the globe brought new products and knowledge about non-Christian societies back to Europe. In a very gradual process that moved by fits and starts, individuals began deciding more for themselves and also gained access to new stimulants such as chocolate, tea, coffee, and sugar. The use of stimulants encouraged the establishment of new social organizations such as coffeehouses, which in turn fostered the proliferation of newspapers and intensified discussion of public issues. In this way, the democratic spiral of expanding selves and societies was set in motion. Internal European factors interacted with global ones; individual choices and experiences prompted new social organizations, which in their turn influenced individual choices and experiences. Both freedom and discipline expanded.[39]

Early modern globalization is an important part of this story, but by itself it explains little, unless we keep in mind that globalization means interdependence and not just interconnection. Globalization developed gradually, as much an outcome of new personal tastes and cultural practices as a facilitator of them. Europeans did not demand exotic goods the instant they were exposed to them; they had to acquire a taste for them—in short, they had to develop personal dispositions and a culture in which they made sense. They reacted initially, whether to coffee or non-European religious practices, with disdain and even horror. As a mock English women's petition against coffee asked in 1674, why did their men "trifle away their *time*, scald their *Chops*, and spend their *Money*, all for a little *base*, *black, thick, nasty, bitter, stinking, nauseous* Puddle water?"[40]

Much remains to be done in explaining how self and society expanded and how that expansion relates to globalization and to democracy as a way of life. Cultural studies in all their varieties have much to say about these questions, and so too do many other forms of inquiry, ranging from economic history to neurohistory. History writing in the global era can only be a collaborative form of inquiry, whether between types of approaches or between scholars from different parts of the globe. We are not just interconnected but also interdependent.

NOTES

INTRODUCTION: HISTORY'S CHANGING FORTUNES

1 *A Catalogue of the Officers and Students of Harvard College for the Academical Year 1852–53. Second Term*, 2nd ed. (Cambridge, MA: John Bartlett, 1853), p. 41 (the catalogue refers only to Worcester's Elements of History and Geography without giving a full reference).

2 *The Study of History in Secondary Schools: Report to the American Historical Association* (New York: Macmillan, 1911), pp. 50–51.

3 "National Assessment of Adult Literacy," Institute of Education Sciences, National Center for Education Statistics, U.S. Department of Education, at http://nces.ed.gov/naal/lit_history.asp (accessed November 4, 2013).

4 For the United States Senate bill, see http://www.gpo.gov/fdsys/pkg/BILLS-111s659is/html/BILLS-111s659is.htm (accessed November 4, 2013).

5 The Ukrainian blueprint for reform is quoted in Catherine Wanner, *Burden of Dreams: History and Identity in Post-Soviet Ukraine* (University Park, PA: Penn State University Press, 1998), p. 82. Titles of courses taught at Taras Shevchenko National Univer-

sity in Kiev are from http://www.history.univ.kiev.ua/en/faculty/history-faculty.html (accessed November 4, 2013).

6   The figures for U.S. history faculty are for the years 2001–2002, from Robert B. Townsend, "State of the History Department: The AHA Annual Department Survey 2001–02," *Perspectives on History*, April 2004, available at http://www.historians.org/publications-and-directories/perspectives-on-history/state-of-the-history-department-the-aha-annual-department-survey-2001-02 (accessed November 4, 2013). The number for Europe has been declining steadily, the numbers for non-Western history have been rising, while the numbers for U.S. history have remained about the same, according to Robert Townsend, "Decline of the West or Rise of the Rest? Data from 2010 Shows Rebalancing of Field Coverage in Departments," *Perspectives on History*, September 2011, available at http://www.historians.org/publications-and-directories/perspectives-on-history/september-2011/decline-of-the-west-or-the-rise-of-the-rest (accessed November 4, 2013). I excluded postdoctoral and research fellows from the count. The figures for Europe can be found in Peter Baldwin, "Smug Britannia: The Dominance of (the) English in Current History Writing and Its Pathologies," *Contemporary European History* 20, Special Issue 3 (2011): 351–366. For the University of Delhi, see http://www.du.ac.in/index.php?id=437&L=0 (consulted August 3, 2012). The Peking University website, however, is less specific than its counterpart in Delhi. It gives no ranks and, in at least one case, lists a historian who recently died at age ninety. See http://web5.pku.edu.cn/en/history/Faculty/ (consulted August 3, 2012). For the Australian National University, see http://history.cass.anu.edu.au/people (consulted August 25, 2012).

7   Table 213, "Enrollment Rates of 18- to 24-Year-Olds in Degree-Granting Institutions, by Level of Institution and Sex and Race/Ethnicity of Student: 1967 through 2010," Digest of Education Statistics, Institute of Education Sciences, National Center for Education Statistics, U.S. Department of Educa-

tion, available at http://nces.ed.gov/programs/digest/d11/tables/dt11_213.asp (accessed November 4, 2013).

8 Rajnarayan Chandavarkar, " 'The Making of the Working Class': E. P. Thompson and Indian History," *History Workshop Journal* 43 (Spring, 1997): 177–196, quote from p. 177.

9 These issues are discussed in greater detail in Joyce Appleby, Lynn Hunt, and Margaret Jacob, *Telling the Truth about History* (New York: W. W. Norton, 1994).

10 Max Weber, *The Theory of Social and Economic Organization*, ed. Talcott Parsons (New York: Free Press, 1964).

CHAPTER ONE: THE RISE AND FALL OF CULTURAL THEORIES

1 Thomas Kuhn, *The Structure of Scientific Revolutions* (Chicago: University of Chicago Press, 1962). See, for example, Joseph F. Musser, "The Perils of Relying on Thomas Kuhn," *Eighteenth-Century Studies* 18 (Winter, 1984–1985): 215–226. For a discussion of paradigms versus turns, see Doris Bachmann-Medick, *Cultural Turns: Neuorientierungen in den Kulturwissenschaften* (Reinbek bei Hamburg: Rowohlt Verlage, 2006).

2 Émile Durkheim, *The Division of Labor in Society* (New York: Free Press, 1984); Max Weber, *From Max Weber: Essays in Sociology*, trans. and ed. H. H. Gerth and C. Wright Mills (Abingdon, UK: Routledge, 1991), p. 128 for "icy darkness."

3 Modernization theory, insofar as it is even a theory, is a huge subject to which I cannot possibly do justice here. See Nils Gilman, *Mandarins of the Future: Modernization Theory in Cold War America* (Baltimore, MD: Johns Hopkins University Press, 2007).

4 R. Colbert Rhodes, "Emile Durkheim and the Historical Thought of Marc Bloch," *Theory and Society* 5, no. 1 (1978): 45–73.

5 The Annales school has been much discussed. See, for example, Stuart Clark, *The Annales School: Histories and Overviews* (London: Taylor & Francis, 1999).

6 Fernand Braudel, *The Mediterranean and the Mediterranean World*

in the Age of Philip II, 2 vols., trans. Siân Reynolds (1949; Berkeley: University of California Press, 1995), quote from vol. 1, p. 21.

7   One of the most influential examples was Emmanuel Le Roy Ladurie, *The Peasants of Languedoc*, trans. John Day (Champaign: University of Illinois Press, 1977).

8   Victoria E. Bonnell and Lynn Hunt, eds., *Beyond the Cultural Turn: New Directions in the Study of Society and Culture* (Berkeley: University of California Press, 1999). For a different view, see *"AHR* Forum: Historiographic 'Turns' in Critical Perspective," *American Historical Review* 117, no. 3 (June, 2012): 698–813.

9   David Morley and Kuan-Hsing Chen, eds., *Stuart Hall: Critical Dialogues in Cultural Studies* (London: Routledge, 1996).

10 Claude Lévi-Strauss, *The Elementary Structures of Kinship*, trans. James Harle Bell and John Richard von Sturmer (1947; Boston: Beacon Press, 1969). For the quote on kinship as language, see François Dosse, *History of Structuralism: The Rising Sign, 1945–1966*, trans. Deborah Glassman (Minneapolis: University of Minnesota Press, 1997). See also Marcel Hénaff, *Claude Lévi-Strauss and the Making of Structural Anthropology*, trans. Mary Baker (Minneapolis: University of Minnesota Press, 1998).

11 Stuart Hall, "Cultural Studies: Two Paradigms," *Media, Culture and Society* 2, no. 1 (January 1, 1980): 57–72.

12 Jacques Derrida, "Structure, Sign, and Play in the Discourse of the Human Sciences [1966]," in Joseph P. Natoli and Linda Hutcheon, eds., *A Postmodern Reader* (Albany, NY: SUNY Press, 1993).

13 A brief and helpful overview can be found in "4. Major Works," in "Michel Foucault," *The Stanford Encyclopedia of Philosophy*, at http://plato.stanford.edu/entries/foucault/#4 (accessed November 6, 2013). An excellent account of the life and work can be found in Jim Miller, *The Passion of Michel Foucault* (Cambridge, MA: Harvard University Press, 1993).

14 Michel Foucault, *The Order of Things: An Archaeology of the Human Sciences* (New York: Pantheon Books, 1970), p. 387; Paul Rabinow, ed., *The Foucault Reader* (New York: Random House, 1984), p. 74.

On Foucault's relationship to Lévi-Strauss, see Miller, *Passion of Michel Foucault*, p. 417.

15 Clifford Geertz, "Thick Description: Toward an Interpretive Theory of Culture," in *The Interpretation of Cultures: Selected Essays* (New York: Basic Books, 1973), p. 14.

16 Joan Wallach Scott, *The Glassworkers of Carmaux: French Craftsmen and Political Action in a Nineteenth-Century City* (Cambridge, MA: Harvard University Press, 1980); Michel de Certeau, Dominique Julia, and Jacques Revel, *Une politique de la langue* (Paris: Gallimard, 1975); Robert J. Corber and Stephen M. Valocchi, *Queer Studies: An Interdisciplinary Reader* (Malden, MA: Wiley-Blackwell, 2003).

17 François Furet, *Penser la Révolution Française* (Paris: Gallimard, 1978), p. 84. See also my discussion in Lynn Hunt, *Politics, Culture, and Class in the French Revolution* (Berkeley: University of California Press, 1984).

18 Gilman, *Mandarins of the Future*.

19 Editors of *Annales*, "History and Social Science: A Critical Turning Point [March–April 1988]," as translated and reproduced in Jacques Revel and Lynn Hunt, eds., *Histories: French Constructions of the Past* (New York: New Press, 1995), pp. 480–483.

20 The most influential work in this regard is Joan Wallach Scott, *Gender and the Politics of History* (New York: Columbia University Press, 1999).

21 Steve Garner, *Whiteness: An Introduction* (New York: Routledge, 2007); Nancy Foner and George M. Fredrickson, *Not Just Black and White: Historical and Contemporary Perspectives on Immigration, Race, and Ethnicity in the United States* (New York: Russell Sage Foundation, 2005), p. 171.

22 Edward Palmer Thompson, *The Making of the English Working Class* (New York: Pantheon Books, 1964), p. 9.

23 Harvey J. Kaye and Keith MacClelland, *E. P. Thompson: Critical Perspectives* (Philadelphia: Temple University Press, 1990); Scott, *Gender and the Politics of History*, pp. 68–92; Anna Clark, *The Strug-*

gle for the Breeches: Gender and the Making of the British Working Class (Berkeley: University of California Press, 1997); E. P. Thompson, *The Poverty of Theory and Other Essays* (New York: Monthly Review Press, 1978).

24   See the figure published in http://blog.historians.org/2009/06/aha-membership-grows-modestly-as-history-of-religion-surpasses-culture/ (accessed November 8, 2013).

25   Philippe Poirrier, *L'Histoire culturelle: un "tournant mondial" dans l'historiographie?* (Dijon: Éditions universitaires de Dijon, 2008); Peter Burke, "Strengths and Weaknesses of Cultural History," *Cultural History* 1, no. 1 (2012): 1–13, p. 1; Michael Payne and Jessica Rae Barbera, eds., *A Dictionary of Cultural and Critical Theory* (Malden, MA: John Wiley, 2010).

26   Dipesh Chakrabarty, *Provincializing Europe: Postcolonial Thought and Historical Difference* (Princeton, NJ: Princeton University Press, 2000), p. 28.

27   Edward W. Said, *Orientalism* (New York: Random House, 1978).

28   For the earlier statement of Chakrabarty's views, see Dipesh Chakrabarty, "Postcoloniality and the Artifice of History: Who Speaks for 'Indian' Pasts?," *Representations* 37 (January 1, 1992): 1–26.

29   Eric Hobsbawm, *Interesting Times: A Twentieth-Century Life* (New York: New Press, 2002), p. 334; Stephen Haber, "Anything Goes: Mexico's 'New' Cultural History," *Hispanic American Historical Review* 79, no. 2 (Special Issue: Mexico's New Cultural History: Una Lucha Libre) (May, 1999): 307–330, quotes from pp. 312, 329.

30   Paula S. Fass, "Cultural History/Social History: Some Reflections on a Continuing Dialogue," *Journal of Social History* 37 (Fall, 2003): 39–46, quote from p. 44.

31   William H. Sewell Jr., "The Concept(s) of Culture," in Bonnell and Hunt, eds., *Beyond the Cultural Turn*, pp. 35–61, quote from p. 36.

32   Richard Biernacki, "Method and Metaphor after the New Cultural History," in Bonnell and Hunt, eds., *Beyond the Cultural Turn*, quote from p. 63; Don Mitchell, "There's No Such Thing as

Culture: Towards a Reconceptualization of the Idea of Culture in Geography," *Transactions of the Institute of British Geographers*, New Series, 20, no. 1 (1995): 102–116.

33 Scott, *Gender and the Politics of History*, p. 4.

34 Laura Lee Downs, "If 'Woman' Is Just an Empty Category, Then Why Am I Afraid to Walk Alone at Night?," *Comparative Studies in Society and History* 35 (April, 1993): 414–437; Joan Hoff, "Gender as a Postmodern Category of Paralysis," *Women's History Review* 3, no. 2 (1994): 149–168.

35 Graham Huggan, "Postcolonialism and Its Discontents," *Transition* 62 (1993): 130–135; Sara Castro-Klaren, "The Latin American Cultural Studies Reader [review]," *MLN* 121, no. 2 (March 28, 2006, Hispanic Issue): 465–472.

36 "Front Matter," *History and Theory* 40, no. 4 (December 1, 2001). For a valiant effort to keep theoretical discussion alive among historians, see Gabrielle M. Spiegel, "The Task of the Historian," *American Historical Review* 114, no. 1 (February, 2009): 1–15. For an example of an introduction to cultural studies, see Chris Rojek, *Cultural Studies* (Cambridge, UK: Polity, 2007). The word "epistemology" does not appear, though Foucault's views on truth are mentioned. More attention is given to concrete topics of cultural studies, for example, reality TV.

37 Tilottama Rajan, "In the Wake of Cultural Studies: Globalization, Theory, and the University," *Diacritics* 31 (Fall, 2001): 67–88, quote from p. 70; Bonnell and Hunt, eds., *Beyond the Cultural Turn*, esp. pp. 10–11.

38 William H. Sewell Jr., *Logics of History: Social Theory and Social Transformation* (Chicago: University of Chicago Press, 2005), quote from p. 77. It is significant that the word "social" appears so prominently in his title.

39 Jean-François Lyotard, *The Postmodern Condition: A Report on Knowledge*, trans. Geoff Bennington and Brian Massumi (Minneapolis: University of Minnesota Press, 1984), quote from p. xxiv.

40 On meta-narratives and postmodernism in general, see Ernst

Breisach, *On the Future of History: The Postmodernist Challenge and Its Aftermath* (Chicago: University of Chicago Press, 2003).

41   On Foucault and Weber, see David Garland, *Punishment and Modern Society: A Study in Social Theory* (Chicago: University of Chicago Press, 1993); Michel Foucault, *Discipline and Punish: The Birth of the Prison* (New York: Random House, 1978), p. 160.

42   Lorraine Code, ed., *Encyclopedia of Feminist Theories* (London: Taylor & Francis, 2000), p. 417. For a critique, see William M. Reddy, "Against Constructionism: The Historical Ethnography of Emotions," *Current Anthropology* 38 (June, 1997): 327–351. See also Tobin Siebers, "Disability in Theory: From Social Constructionism to the New Realism of the Body," *American Literary History* 13 (Winter, 2001): 737–775.

CHAPTER TWO: THE CHALLENGE OF GLOBALIZATION

1   Titles using the American (globalization) and those using the British (globalisation) spelling were combined. Since WorldCat is constantly being updated, it is important to note that this graph reflects the state of the catalogue in October 2013. The data end in 2009 because constant updating of the catalogue makes the most recent years the least reliable (the most liable to have books added). A graph based on articles might give a more nuanced picture. According to Michael Lang, interest in globalization first peaked among those studying business in the late 1970s and early 1980s. Michael Lang, "Globalization and Its History," *Journal of Modern History* 78, no. 4 (2006): 899–931. I broached some of the questions about globalization in Lynn Hunt, "Globalisation and Time," in Chris Lorenz and Berber Bevernage, eds., *Breaking Up Time: Negotiating the Borders between Present, Past, and Future* (Schriftenreihe der FRIAS School of History, vol. 7) (Göttingen: Vandenhoeck & Ruprecht, 2013), pp. 199–215.

2   Claude E. Barfield, Günter Heiduk, and Paul J. J. Welfens, eds., *Internet, Economic Growth and Globalization: Perspectives on the New*

Economy in Europe, Japan and the USA (Berlin: Springer, 2003). On Internet usage, see Internet World Stats, Usage and Population Statistics, http://www.internetworldstats.com/stats.htm (accessed November 8, 2013).

3 Anthony Giddens made this argument in his BBC Reith Lectures of 1999, available at http://news.bbc.co.uk/hi/english/static/events/reith_99/week1/week1.htm (accessed November 8, 2013).

4 The literature on globalization is enormous and cannot be summarized here. For an influential Marxist view, see Michael Hardt and Antonio Negri, *Empire* (Cambridge, MA: Harvard University Press, 2001).

5 *Nous sommes des sang-mêlés: manuel d'histoire de la civilisation Française*, Lucien Febvre and François Crouzet, ed. Denis and Elisabeth Crouzet (Paris: Albin Michel, 2012). I am grateful to Caroline Ford for drawing my attention to this work and sharing her review of it. Some of the original textbook can be found in the archives of UNESCO at http://www.unesco.org/new/en/unesco/resources/online-materials/publications/unesdoc-database/ (the typewritten UNESCO document is dated December 28, 1951; accessed November 8, 2013).

6 Lynn Avery Hunt, *Revolution and Urban Politics in Provincial France: Troyes and Reims, 1786–1790* (Stanford: Stanford University Press, 1978).

7 Gilbert Allardyce, "Toward World History: American Historians and the Coming of the World History Course," *Journal of World History* 1, no. 1 (1990): 23–76; Sharon Cohen, *AP World History Teacher's Guide* (New York: College Board, 2007), quote from p. 1, available at http://www.google.com/url?sa=t&rct=j&q=&esrc=s&source=web&cd=1&ved=0CCwQFjAA&url=http%3A%2F%2Fapcentral.collegeboard.com%2Fapc%2Fmembers%2Freposito ry%2Fap07_worldhist_teachersguide.pdf&ei=A3LxUbrJLsq niAKWmoGgCg&usg=AFQjCNEXjZ3RNWL_fJtth1GGi6N_UeyvaA&bvm=bv.49784469,d.cGE (accessed November 8, 2013).

8 Subarticle 3 of article 14 of Recommendation 1283, p. 53 of *The*

Challenges of the Information and Communication Technologies Facing History Teaching (Symposium, March 25–27, 1999, Andorra la Vella [Andorra]), ed. Jacques Tardif (Strasbourg: Council of Europe, 1999).

9   For an excellent overview of world and global history around the world, see Pierre Grosser, "L'Histoire mondiale/globale, une jeunesse exubérante mais difficile," *Vingtième Siècle. Revue d'histoire* 110, no. 2 (2011): 3–18.

10 On the states of the former Yugoslavia, see, for example, the European Association of History Educators, "History That Connects the Western Balkans," http://www.euroclio.eu/new/index.php/work/history-that-connects (accessed November 9, 2013).

11 For a general view on the transnational turn in U.S. history, see Thomas Bender, *A Nation among Nations: America's Place in World History* (New York: Hill & Wang, 2006). For an excellent example of the kind of research that is being undertaken, see Carla Gardina Pestana, *Protestant Empire: Religion and the Making of the British Atlantic World* (Philadelphia: University of Pennsylvania Press, 2009). On slavery, see Robin Blackburn, *The Overthrow of Colonial Slavery, 1776–1848* (London: Verso, 1988); Ina Baghdiantz McCabe, *Orientalism in Early Modern France: Eurasian Trade, Exoticism, and the Ancien Régime* (New York: Berg, 2008); Eugen Weber, *Peasants into Frenchmen: The Modernization of Rural France, 1870–1914* (Stanford: Stanford University Press, 1976).

12 In an influential definition, Robert Keohane and Joseph Nye maintain that globalization is an increase in globalism, which they equate with "networks of interdependence at multi-continental distances." Joseph S. Nye and Robert O. Keohane, "Globalization: What's New, What's Not (and So What)?," in Joseph S. Nye, *Power in the Global Information Age: From Realism to Globalization* (London: Routledge, 2004), p. 191.

13 The question of whether globalization constitutes a paradigm has already generated a considerable literature. See, for example, Philip G. Cerny, "Globalization and Other Stories: The Search for a New Paradigm for International Relations," *International Journal* 51, no. 4 (1996): 617–637.

14 Arjun Appadurai, ed., *Globalization* (Durham, NC: Duke University Press, 2001), p. 4.

15 For an emphasis on deterritorialization, see Jan Aart Scholte, *Globalization: A Critical Introduction* (Houndmills, Basingstoke, Hampshire, UK: Palgrave Macmillan, 2000).

16 Anthony Giddens, "The Globalizing of Modernity [originally published 1990]," in David Held and Anthony G. McGrew, eds., *The Global Transformations Reader: An Introduction to the Globalization Debate*, 2nd ed. (London: Wiley-Blackwell, 2003), p. 60. The passage from *The Communist Manifesto* can be found at http://www.gutenberg.org/files/61/61.txt.

17 Cátia Antunes, "Globalisation in History and the History of Globalisation: The Application of a Globalisation Model to Historical Research," in William R. Thompson, George Modelski, and Tessaleno Devesas, eds., *Globalization as Evolutionary Process: Modeling Global Change* (London: Taylor & Francis, 2008), pp. 242–266. Other names have been cited but Braudel, Wallerstein, and Frank do invariably come up for discussion. See, for example, Krzysztof Pomian, "World History: histoire mondiale, histoire universelle," *Le Débat* 154, no. 2 (2009): 14–40; Olivier Pétré-Grenouilleau, "La Galaxie histoire-monde," *Le Débat* 154, no. 2 (2009): 41–52.

18 Fernand Braudel, *Civilization and Capitalism, 15th–18th Century*, vol. 1: *The Structure of Everyday Life* (Berkeley: University of California Press, 1992), p. 562.

19 Immanuel Wallerstein, *World-Systems Analysis: An Introduction* (Durham, NC: Duke University Press, 2004), pp. x, 23. Wallerstein began his project with *Modern World-System I: Capitalist Agriculture and the Origins of the European World-Economy in the Sixteenth Century (Studies in Social Discontinuity)* (New York: Academic Press, 1974).

20 Andre Gunder Frank, *ReORIENT: Global Economy in the Asian Age* (Berkeley: University of California Press, 1998).

21 Arjun Appadurai, "Disjuncture and Difference in the Global Cultural Economy," *Public Culture* 2, no. 2 (Spring, 1990): 1–24, p. 7; Arjun Appadurai, "Global Ethnoscapes: Notes and Queries

for a Transnational Anthropology," in R. G. Fox, ed., *Recapturing Anthropology: Working in the Present* (Santa Fe: School of American Research, 1991), pp. 191–210; Gabriel Ignatow, *Transnational Identity Politics and the Environment* (Lanham, MD: Rowman & Littlefield, 2007), quote from p. 34.

22 For the specializations of French historians in 2000, see the remarks of Bernard Thomann, "Histoire et mondialisation," *idées. fr*, October 2, 2008, at http://www.laviedesidees.fr/Histoire-et-mondialisation,449.html (viewed August 24, 2012); and also the introduction by Caroline Douki and Philippe Minard, "Histoire globale, histoires connectées: un changement d'échelle historiographique?," *Revue d'histoire moderne et contemporaine*, 54, no. 4 (2007): 7–21.

23 Jerry H. Bentley, "Globalizing History and Historicizing Globalization," *Globalizations* 1, no. 1 (2004): 69–81, quote from p. 79.

24 Patrick O'Brien, "Historiographical Traditions and Modern Imperatives for the Restoration of Global History," *Journal of Global History* 1 (2006): 3–39, quote from p. 37.

25 John M. Hobson, *The Eastern Origins of Western Civilisation* (Cambridge, UK: Cambridge University Press, 2004), quote from p. 2 and Contents.

26 Anibal Quijano (Michael Ennis, trans.), "Coloniality of Power, Eurocentrism, and Latin America," *Nepantla: Views from South* 1 (2000): 533–580, quote from p. 552.

27 Ibid., especially p. 537.

28 Sanjay Subrahmanyam, "Connected Histories: Notes towards a Reconfiguration of Early Modern Eurasia," *Modern Asian Studies* 31, no. 3 (July 1, 1997): 735–762, quote from p. 745. Rostow was a leading modernization theorist.

29 Charles Edquist and Leif Hommen, eds., *Small Country Innovation Systems: Globalization, Change and Policy in Asia and Europe* (Cheltenham, UK: Edward Elgar, 2008), pp. 8, 486. On growthmanship, see David C. Engerman, "Bernath Lecture: American Knowledge and Global Power," *Diplomatic History* 31, no. 4 (2007): 599–622.

30 Kären Wigen, "Cartographies of Connection: Ocean Maps as

Metaphors for Interarea History," in Jerry H. Bentley, Renate Bridenthal, and Anand A. Yang, eds., *Interactions: Transregional Perspectives on World History* (Honolulu: University of Hawai'i Press, 2005); W. Jeffrey Bolster, "Putting the Ocean in Atlantic History: Maritime Communities and Marine Ecology in the Northwest Atlantic, 1500–1800," *American Historical Review* 113, no. 1 (February, 2008): 19–47.

31 Morten Jerven, "An Unlevel Playing Field: National Income Estimates and Reciprocal Comparison in Global Economic History," *Journal of Global History* 7 (2012): 107–128. The other articles mentioned here can be found in the same issue.

32 Marcy Norton, *Sacred Gifts, Profane Pleasures: A History of Tobacco and Chocolate in the Atlantic World* (Ithaca, NY: Cornell University Press, 2010).

33 Francesca Trivellato, *The Familiarity of Strangers: The Sephardic Diaspora, Livorno, and Cross-Cultural Trade in the Early Modern Period* (New Haven, CT: Yale University Press, 2009); Sebouh David Aslanian, *From the Indian Ocean to the Mediterranean: The Global Trade Networks of Armenian Merchants from New Julfa* (Berkeley: University of California Press, 2011); Claude Markovits, *The Global World of Indian Merchants, 1750–1947: Traders of Sind from Bukhara to Panama* (Cambridge, UK: Cambridge University Press, 2000). On the Scots, see the fascinating family study by Emma Rothschild, *The Inner Life of Empires: An Eighteenth-Century History* (Princeton, NJ: Princeton University Press, 2011).

34 Sarah Abrevaya Stein, *Plumes: Ostrich Feathers, Jews, and a Lost World of Global Commerce* (New Haven, CT: Yale University Press, 2008), p. 7.

35 Markovits, *Global World of Indian Merchants*; Aslanian, *Indian Ocean to the Mediterranean*; Graziano Krätli and Ghislaine Lydon, eds., *The Trans-Saharan Book Trade: Manuscript Culture, Arabic Literacy and Intellectual History in Muslim Africa* (Leiden: Brill, 2011); Giorgio Riello and Tirthankar Roy, eds., *How India Clothed the World: The World of South Asian Textiles, 1500–1850* (Leiden: Brill, 2009).

36 *Knowledge, Networks and Nations: Global Scientific Collaboration in*

the Twenty-First Century (London: Royal Society, 2011), esp. p. 17. The figures are based on peer-reviewed literature in science, technology, medicine, the social sciences, the arts, and the humanities.

37 Walter D. Mignolo, "The Geopolitics of Knowledge and the Colonial Difference," *South Atlantic Quarterly* 101, no. 1 (2002): 57–96, quotes from pp. 49, 90.

38 For a rejection of Western-style research and analysis, see Ashis Nandy, "History's Forgotten Doubles," *History and Theory* 34, no. 2 (Theme Issue 34: World Historians and Their Critics) (May, 1995): 44–66. On the supposedly Eurocentric elements, see the screed by Jack Goody, *The Theft of History* (New York: Cambridge University Press, 2006). Dipesh Chakrabarty, *Provincializing Europe: Postcolonial Thought and Historical Difference* (Princeton, NJ: Princeton University Press, 2001), p. 41. For an example of the varieties of history, see Velcheru Narayana Rao et al., *Textures of Time: Writing History in South India* (Ann Arbor, MI: Other Press, 2003).

39 For an analysis of the language of globalization, see Geoff Eley, "Historicizing the Global, Politicizing Capital: Giving the Present a Name," *History Workshop Journal* 63 (Spring, 2007): 154–188. A reply to some of Eley's points is given by Sanjay Subrahmanyam, "Historicizing the Global, or Labouring for Invention?," *History Workshop Journal* 64, no. 1 (2007): 329–334. For the influence of globalization on religion, see Renato Ortiz, "Notes on Religion and Globalization," *Nepantla: Views from South* 4, no. 3 (2003): 423–448. On Buddhism, see Brian Peter Harvey, *An Introduction to Buddhism: Teachings, History, and Practices* (Cambridge, UK: Cambridge University Press, 1990), esp. pp. 139–169.

40 Benedict Anderson, *Imagined Communities: Reflections on the Origin and Spread of Nationalism*, rev. ed. (1983; London: Verso, 1999), p. 4.

41 See the special forum "Alberto Banti's Interpretation of Risorgimento Nationalism: A Debate," *Nations and Nationalism* 15 (July, 2009): 396–460.

42 On the import of the 1820s for globalization, see Adam McKeown, "Periodizing Globalization," *History Workshop Journal* 63 (Spring,

2007): 218–230. On the current relationship between globalization and nationalism, see Mary Kaldor, "Nationalism and Globalisation," *Nations and Nationalism* 10 (2004): 161–177. She emphasizes the two-way relationship, that is, new forms of nationalism affect the forms that globalization will take.

43 Pascale Casanova, *The World Republic of Letters*, trans. M. B. DeBevoise (Cambridge, MA: Harvard University Press, 2005), p. 40. These thoughts are further developed in Pascale Casanova, "Literature as a World," *New Left Review* 31 (January–February, 2005): 71–90, quote from p. 72.

44 For a more transnational approach to global cinematic culture, see Vanessa R. Schwartz, *It's So French! Hollywood, Paris, and the Making of Cosmopolitan Film Culture* (Chicago: University of Chicago Press, 2007).

45 The concluding sentence of Trivellato's wonderful study *The Familiarity of Strangers* is indicative of both the limitations and the potential of what has been done so far: "I have suggested that we turn to these phenomena not as metahistorical recurrences, nor as unique marvels of intragroup solidarity, nor as relics of primordial forms of capitalism, but as complex organizations that shed light on multifarious processes of social and economic change and thus also test the role and limits of the market in transforming early modern societies." (p. 278)

CHAPTER 3: RETHINKING SOCIETY AND THE SELF

1 There are exceptions to the neglect, but even the small signs of interest in rethinking the social are not accompanied by any connection to the self. See, for example, Patrick Joyce, ed., *The Social in Question: New Bearings in History and the Social Sciences* (London: Routledge, 2002); Jean Terrier, *Visions of the Social: Society as a Political Project in France, 1750–1950* (Leiden: Brill, 2011).

2 Writing of the history of sexuality, Foucault claimed, "It was during the same period—the end of the eighteenth century—and

for reasons that will have to be determined, that there emerged a completely new technology of sex." Michel Foucault, *The History of Sexuality*, vol. 1: *An Introduction*, trans. Robert Hurley (New York: Pantheon Books, 1978), p. 116.

3   Michel Foucault and Colin Gordon, *Power/Knowledge: Selected Interviews and Other Writings, 1972–1977* (New York: Pantheon Books, 1980), p. 98. Guides to the terrain can be found in Charles Taylor, *Sources of the Self: The Making of the Modern Identity* (Cambridge, MA: Harvard University Press, 1989); Jerrold Seigel, *The Idea of the Self: Thought and Experience in Western Europe since the Seventeenth Century* (Cambridge, UK: Cambridge University Press, 2005).

4   Eric J. Evans, *Thatcher and Thatcherism*, 2nd ed. (London: Routledge, 2004), p. 137.

5   I base these conclusions on the *Oxford English Dictionary* and the various French dictionaries made available by the ARTFL Project. Most helpful on this question is Keith Michael Baker, "Enlightenment and the Institution of Society: Notes for a Conceptual History," in Sudipta Kaviraj and Sunil Khilnani, eds., *Civil Society: History and Possibilities* (Cambridge, UK: Cambridge University Press, 2001), pp. 84–104.

6   The quote comes from *Encyclopédie*, vol. 15, p. 251, as provided by the ARTFL Project: http://artflsrv02.uchicago.edu/cgi-bin/extras/encpageturn.pl?V15/ENC_15-251.jpeg (consulted August 7, 2013).

7   For the definition of "*philosophe*" in *Encyclopédie*, vol. 12, p. 510, see http://artflsrv02.uchicago.edu/cgi-bin/extras/encpageturn.pl?V15/ENC_15-251.jpeg (consulted August 7, 2013). The anonymous pamphlet of 1743 is discussed in Margaret Jacob, "The Clandestine Universe of Early Eighteenth Century," December 6, 2001, available at http://www.pierre-marteau.com/c/jacob/clandestine.html (consulted August 7, 2013).

8   *Encyclopédie*, vol. 12, p. 510, at http://artflsrv02.uchicago.edu/cgi-bin/extras/encpageturn.pl?V15/ENC_15-251.jpeg (consulted August 7, 2013).

9   Émile Durkheim, *Les formes élémentaires de la vie religieuse. Le système totémique en Australie*, 5th ed. (Paris: Les Presses universitaires de France, 1968), quotes from pp. 203, 209.

10 The subject of secularization is immense and much too often studied exclusively in the context of Christianity and developments in the West. See, for example, Marcel Gauchet, *The Disenchantment of the World*, trans. Oscar Burge (Princeton, NJ: Princeton University Press, 1997).

11 Robert Wokler, "Saint-Simon and the Passage from Political to Social Science," in Anthony Robin Pagden, ed., *The Languages of Political Theory in Early-Modern Europe* (Cambridge, UK: Cambridge University Press, 1990), pp. 325–338.

12 Charles John Sommerville, *The News Revolution in England: Cultural Dynamics of Daily Information* (New York: Oxford University Press, 1996), p. 77.

13 For Millar's use of the term "modern European nations," see John Millar, *Observations concerning the Origin of the Distinction of the Ranks in Society*, 2nd ed. (London: J. Murray, 1773), p. 298. On civil society, see Sudipta Kaviraj and Sunil Khilnani, eds., *Civil Society: History and Possibilities* (Cambridge, UK: Cambridge University Press, 2001).

14 Raymond Williams, *Culture and Society, 1780–1950* (first published 1958; New York: Columbia University Press, 1983), p. xv. On sociology, see *Oxford English Dictionary* at http://www.oed.com /view/Entry/183792?redirectedFrom=sociology#eid (consulted September 13, 2012). Jacques Guilhaumou has traced the invention of the term "*sociologie*" to Abbé Sieyès around the time of the French Revolution of 1789. "Sieyès et le non-dit de la sociologie: du mot à la chose," *Revue d'histoire des sciences humaines, Naissance de la science sociale (1750–1850)*, 15 (2006): 117–134.

15 For histories of the concept of society, see Brian C. J. Singer, *Society, Theory and the French Revolution: Studies in the Revolutionary Imaginary* (New York: Macmillan, 1986); Terrier, *Visions of the Social.*

16 World Bank, *Building Knowledge Economies: Advanced Strategies for*

Development (Washington, DC: World Bank Publications, 2007), p. 23. The literature on knowledge economies is growing by leaps and bounds. See, for example, John H. Dunning, ed., *Regions, Globalization, and the Knowledge-Based Economy* (Oxford, UK: Oxford University Press, 2000).

17 David Harvey, *The Condition of Postmodernity: An Enquiry into the Origins of Cultural Change* (Cambridge, MA: Basil Blackwell, 1989), esp. p. 247. The 1968 definition is cited in Peter Wagner, " 'An Entire New Object of Consciousness, of Volition, of Thought': The Coming into Being and (Almost) Passing Away of 'Society' as a Scientific Object," in Lorraine Daston, ed., *Biographies of Scientific Objects* (Chicago: University of Chicago Press, 2000), pp. 132–157, quote from p. 150.

18 John Urry, *Sociology beyond Societies: Mobilities for the Twenty-First Century* (London: Routledge, 2000).

19 Daniel Lord Smail, *On Deep History and the Brain* (Berkeley: University of California Press, 2008). On Darwin and the social instinct, see Darrin M. McMahon, *Happiness: A History* (New York: Atlantic Monthly Press, 2006), p. 417.

20 Harriet Ritvo, *The Animal Estate: The English and Other Creatures in the Victorian Age* (Cambridge, MA: Harvard University Press, 1987).

21 Edward Payson Evans, *The Criminal Prosecution and Capital Punishment of Animals* (London: W. Heinemann, 1906), p. 186; Linda Kalof and Brigitte Resl, eds., *A Cultural History of Animals*, 6 vols. (Oxford, UK: Berg, 2007); Harriet Ritvo, "Humans and Humanists," *Daedalus* (Summer, 2009): 68–78.

22 See "World Declaration on Primates," http://www.projetogap.org.br/en/world-declaration-on-great-primates/ (consulted November 10, 2013); Chimpanzee Sequencing and Analysis Consortium, "Initial Sequence of the Chimpanzee Genome and Comparison with the Human Genome," *Nature* 437, no. 7055 (September 1, 2005): 69–87; Kay Prüfer et al., "The Bonobo Genome Compared with the Chimpanzee and Human Genomes," *Nature* (June 13,

2012), http://www.nature.com/nature/journal/vaop/ncurrent/full/nature11128.html (consulted August 15, 2013).

23   Robert J. Losey et al., "Canids as Persons: Early Neolithic Dog and Wolf Burials, Cis-Baikal, Siberia," *Journal of Anthropological Archaeology* 30, no. 2 (June, 2011): 174–189; Donna J. Haraway, *When Species Meet* (Minneapolis: University of Minnesota Press, 2007).

24   Dorothee Brantz, "The Natural Space of Modernity: A Transatlantic Perspective on (Urban) Environmental History," in Ursula Lehmkuhl and Hermann Wellenreuther, eds., *Historians and Nature: Comparative Approaches to Environmental History* (Oxford, UK: Berg, 2007), pp. 195–225. See also Haraway, *When Species Meet.*

25   Dipesh Chakrabarty, "The Climate of History: Four Theses," *Critical Inquiry* 35 (Winter, 2009): 197–222; Dipesh Chakrabarty, "Postcolonial Studies and the Challenge of Climate Change," *New Literary History* 43, no. 1 (2012): 1–18.

26   N. Katherine Hayles, *How We Became Posthuman: Virtual Bodies in Cybernetics, Literature, and Informatics* (Chicago: University of Chicago Press, 1999).

27   Paul Glennie and Nigel Thrift, *Shaping the Day: A History of Timekeeping in England and Wales 1300–1800* (Oxford, UK: Oxford University Press, 2009).

28   Wilfred Cantwell Smith, "American Academy of Religion, Annual Meeting 1983: The Presidential Address. The Modern West in the History of Religion," *Journal of the American Academy of Religion* 52, no. 1 (March, 1984): 3–18, quotes from pp. 9, 10.

29   Dipesh Chakrabarty, *Provincializing Europe: Postcolonial Thought and Historical Difference* (Princeton, NJ: Princeton University Press, 2000), quote from p. 89. For the thematic interests of historians in the United States, see Robert Townsend, "A New Found Religion: The Field Surges among AHA Members," *Perspectives on History* (December, 2009), available at http://www.historians.org/perspectives/issues/2009/0912/0912new3.cfm (consulted Septem-

ber 14, 2012). The numbers are small (7.7 percent for religion, 7.5 percent for cultural history) because the range of categories is so large.

30 On maps, see Paul Rodaway, *Sensuous Geographies: Body, Sense, and Place* (London: Routledge, 1994), esp. pp. 133–142. Lynn Hunt, *Measuring Time, Making History* (Budapest: Central European University, 2008).

31 Paul de Gaudemar, "Le concept de socialisation dans la sociologie de l'éducation chez Durkheim," in W. S. F. Pickering, ed., *Emile Durkheim: Critical Assessments of Leading Sociologists* (London: Taylor & Francis, 2001), pp. 396–403.

32 For a recent exposition of these views, see Charles Zastrow and Karen K. Kirst-Ashman, *Understanding Human Behavior and the Social Environment*, 8th ed. (Belmont, CA: Cengage Learning, 2010).

33 Joan Scott, "The Evidence of Experience," *Critical Inquiry* 17 (1991): quotes from pp. 779, 793.

34 Norbert Elias, *The Civilizing Process: The Development of Manners*, trans. Edmund Jephcott (original German edition, 1939; New York: Urizen Books, 1978).

35 See ibid., esp. p. 201. For a trenchant critique of Elias's views of the Middle Ages, see Barbara H. Rosenwein, "Worrying about Emotions in History," *American Historical Review* 107, no. 3 (June, 2002): 821–845.

36 Lucien Febvre, "La sensibilité et l'histoire: comment reconstituer la vie affective d'autrefois?" *Annales d'histoire sociale* 3 (January–June, 1941): 5–20, quote from p. 9; René van der Veer, "Henri Wallon's Theory of Early Child Development: The Role of Emotions," *Developmental Review* 16, no. 4 (December, 1996): 364–390. For another view of the models of Elias and Febvre, see Jakob Tanner, "Unfassbare Gefühle: Emotionen in der Geistwissenschaft vom *Fin de siècle* bis in die Zwischenkriegzeit," in Uffa Jensen and Daniel Morat, eds., *Rationalisierungen des Gefühls. Zum Verhältnis von Wissenschaft und Emotionen* (Munich: Wilhelm Fink Verlag, 2008), pp. 35–59.

37 Alphonse Dupront, "Problèmes et méthodes d'une histoire de la psychologie collective," *Annales: economies, sociétés, civilisations* 16 (1961): 3–11.

38 Lloyd de Mause, "The Independence of Psychohistory," in Geoffrey Cocks and Travis L. Crosby, eds., *Psycho/history: Readings in the Method of Psychology, Psychoanalysis, and History* (New Haven, CT: Yale University Press, 1987), pp. 50–67, quote from p. 50. For an especially harsh critique of psychohistory, see David E. Stannard, *Shrinking History: On Freud and the Failure of Psychohistory* (New York: Oxford University Press, 1980).

39 Gustave Le Bon, *The Crowd: A Study of the Popular Mind* (New York: Macmillan, 1896), quotes from pp. 13, 17, 109. See also Susanna Barrows, *Distorting Mirrors: Visions of the Crowd in Late Nineteenth-Century France* (New Haven, CT: Yale University Press, 1981), esp. p. 169.

40 Alfred Stein, "Adolf Hitler und G. Le Bon: der Meister des Massenbewegung und sein Lehrer," *Geschichte in Wissenschaft und Unterricht* 6 (1955): 362–368; George Rudé, *The Crowd in History: A Study of Popular Disturbances in France and England, 1730–1848* (New York: Wiley, 1964).

41 Edward Palmer Thompson, *The Making of the English Working Class* (New York: Pantheon Books, 1964), esp. pp. 375–381.

42 As quoted in Robert M. Strozier, *Foucault, Subjectivity, and Identity: Historical Constructions of Subject and Self* (Detroit, MI: Wayne State University Press, 2002), p. 70 (from an interview with Foucault published in 1979).

43 I have found especially helpful the critique developed in Lyndal Roper, *Oedipus and the Devil: Witchcraft, Sexuality, and Religion in Early Modern Europe* (London: Routledge, 1994).

44 William L. Langer, "The Next Assignment," *American Historical Review* 63, no. 2 (January, 1958): 283–304. On the contemporary view of psychoanalysis, see, for example, Peter Brooks and Alex Woloch, eds., *Whose Freud? The Place of Psychoanalysis in Contemporary Culture* (New Haven, CT: Yale University Press, 2000); Eric R. Kandel, *The Age of Insight: The Quest to Understand the Uncon-*

scious in Art, Mind, and Brain: From Vienna 1900 to the Present, 1st ed. (New York: Random House, 2012).

45   Roy F. Baumeister, "The Self," in Daniel T. Gilbert, Susan T. Fiske, and Gardner Lindzey, eds., *The Handbook of Social Psychology*, 4th ed., vol. 1 (Boston: McGraw-Hill, 1998), pp. 680–740, quote from p. 680. A more positive tone, emphasizing the recovery of interest in the self, can be heard in the recent version of the handbook, William B. Swann Jr. and Jennifer K. Bosson, "Self and Identity," in Susan T. Fiske, Daniel T. Gilbert, and Gardner Lindzey, eds., *Handbook of Social Psychology*, 5th ed., vol. 1 (Hoboken, NJ: John Wiley, 2010), pp. 589–628.

46   Michael S. Gazzaniga, *The Mind's Past* (Berkeley: University of California Press, 1998), p. xi; Michael S. Gazzaniga, "Forty-Five Years of Split-Brain Research and Still Going Strong," *Nature Reviews Neuroscience* 6, no. 8 (August 1, 2005): 653–659, quotes from pp. 657, 658.

47   William M. Reddy, *The Navigation of Feeling: A Framework for the History of Emotions* (Cambridge, UK: Cambridge University Press, 2001).

48   Barbara H. Rosenwein, *Emotional Communities in the Early Middle Ages* (Ithaca, NY: Cornell University Press, 2006). The key figure on universality of emotional expression is Paul Ekman. See, for example, Charles Darwin, *The Expression of the Emotions in Man and Animals*, intro. and commentaries by Paul Ekman, essay on the history of the illustrations by Philip Prodger (Oxford, UK: Oxford University Press, 2002). For a critical overview of historians' rather limited interest in emotions and neuroscience, see Rafael Mandressi, "Le Temps profond et le temps perdu," *Revue d'histoire des sciences humaines* 25, no. 2 (2011): 167–204.

49   Antonio R. Damasio, *Descartes' Error: Emotion, Reason, and the Human Brain* (New York: G. P. Putnam's Sons, 1994). See also Damasio's *Feeling of What Happens: Body and Emotion in the Making of Consciousness* (New York: Harcourt, 1999). On affective sciences, see John Protevi, *Political Affect: Connecting the Social and the*

Somatic (Minneapolis: University of Minnesota Press, 2009), p. 23. For the implications for historical analysis, see William M. Reddy, "Saying Something New: Practice Theory and Cognitive Neuroscience," *Arcadia—International Journal for Literary Studies* 44, no. 1 (2009): 8–23.

50 Elias, *Civilizing Process*; Rosenwein, *Emotional Communities*; Jan Plamper, "The History of Emotions: An Interview with William Reddy, Barbara Rosenwein, and Peter Stearns," *History and Theory* 49, no. 2 (2010): 237–265; Ute Frevert, *Emotions in History—Lost and Found* (Budapest: Central European University Press, 2011). For the best overview, see Monique Scheer, "Are Emotions a Kind of Practice (and Is That What Makes Them Have a History?): A Bourdieuian Approach to Understanding Emotion," *History and Theory* 51, no. 2 (2012): 193–220.

51 Antonio Damasio, *Self Comes to Mind: Constructing the Conscious Brain* (New York: Vintage Books, 2010), p. 193; Damasio, *Descartes' Error*, pp. 238–239.

52 Damasio, *Self Comes to Mind*, pp. 196–197.

53 John R. Searle, "The Mystery of Consciousness Continues," *New York Review of Books* (June 9, 2011), available at http://www.nybooks.com/articles/archives/2011/jun/09/mystery-consciousness-continues/?pagination=false (accessed November 10, 2013). It is worth noting that Mikkel Borch-Jakobsen similarly criticized Freud for assuming the consciousness of the ego in order to explain its emergence: "How is it that I may have a relation to my body as *my body*, my *own* body, if it is not by saying 'I,' 'me,' 'ego,' *Ich*? . . . Are we not dealing, much more probably, with the ego-agency, with that ego which Freud admitted he had not 'sufficiently studied?' " Mikkel Borch-Jacobsen, *The Freudian Subject* (Stanford: Stanford University Press, 1989), pp. 70–71.

54 Searle, "Mystery of Consciousness Continues."

55 F. J. Varela, E. Thompson, and E. Rosch. *The Embodied Mind: Cognitive Science and Human Experience* (Cambridge, MA: MIT Press, 1991), p. 14, as quoted in Zoe Drayson, "Embodied Cognitive Sci-

ence and Its Implications for Psychopathology," *Philosophy, Psychiatry, and Psychology* 16, no. 4 (2009): 329–334, quote from p. 331.

56   On the influence of Merleau-Ponty, see, for example, George Lakoff and Mark Johnson, *Philosophy in the Flesh: The Embodied Mind and Its Challenge to Western Thought* (New York: Basic Books, 1999), p. xi. On the body schema, see Ted Toadvine and Leonard Lawlor, eds., *The Merleau-Ponty Reader* (Evanston, IL: Northwestern University Press, 2007), p. 147.

57   Damasio, *Self Comes to Mind*, p. 93. See, for example, Lakoff and Johnson, *Philosophy in the Flesh* (p. 266): Other than insisting that "what we call 'mind' is really embodied," their definitions of mind remain vague, as in "mind isn't some mysterious abstract entity that we bring to bear on our experience. Rather, mind is part of the very structure and fabric of our interactions with our world."

58   Shaun Gallagher, *How the Body Shapes the Mind* (Oxford, UK: Clarendon Press, 2005), pp. 65–78. Damasio and Gallagher cite each other's work but without much extended discussion. See ibid., pp. 135–137.

59   I use the expression "embodied self" rather than "mindful body" because there is much more writing—in a variety of fields— contesting the universality of selves (of personhood, of individuation) than there is challenging the universality of bodies. Nancy Scheper-Hughes and Margaret M. Lock, "The Mindful Body: A Prolegomenon to Future Work in Medical Anthropology," *Medical Anthropology Quarterly*, New Series, 1, no. 1 (March 1, 1987): 6–41; M. R. Bennett and Peter Michael Stephan Hacker, *Philosophical Foundations of Neuroscience* (Malden, MA: Blackwell, 2003), pp. 68–73.

60   Hanne De Jaegher, Ezequiel Di Paolo, and Shaun Gallagher, "Can Social Interaction Constitute Social Cognition?" *Trends in Cognitive Sciences* 14, no. 10 (October 1, 2010): 441–447. "Social neuroscience" uses neuroscientific techniques to get at the brain functions that underlay behavior, rather than studying how social interactions shape neurological development itself. See, for exam-

ple, Tiffany A. Ito, "Implicit Social Cognition: Insights from Social Neuroscience," in Bertram Gawronski and B. Keith Payne, eds., *Handbook of Implicit Social Cognition: Measurement, Theory, and Applications* (New York: Guilford Press, 2011), pp. 80–92.

61 Some useful distinctions are developed in Diana Coole, "Rethinking Agency: A Phenomenological Approach to Embodiment and Agentic Capacities," *Political Studies* 53, no. 1 (2005): 124–142.

62 Mehdi Moussaïd, Dirk Helbing, and Guy Theraulaz, "How Simple Rules Determine Pedestrian Behavior and Crowd Disasters," *Proceedings of the National Academy of Sciences of the United States of America*, 108, no. 17 (April 26, 2011): 6884-6888, available at http://www.pnas.org/content/early/2011/04/08/1016507108 (consulted September 19, 2012).

CHAPTER FOUR: NEW PURPOSES, NEW PARADIGMS

1 See, for example, Kenneth Pomeranz, *The Great Divergence: China, Europe, and the Making of the Modern World Economy* (Princeton, NJ: Princeton University Press, 2009).

2 Declaration of Independence, available at http://www.archives.gov/exhibits/charters/declaration_transcript.html (accessed November 11, 2013).

3 Kay Young and Jeffrey L. Saver, "The Neurology of Narrative," *SubStance* 30 (2001): 72–84; Richard M. Lerner, *Handbook of Child Psychology: Theoretical Models of Human Development*, vol. 1, of William Damon and Richard M. Lerner, eds., *Handbook of Child Psychology*, 6th ed. (Hoboken, NJ: John Wiley, 2006), p. 744.

4 For the Barthes quote, see Martin McQuillan, ed., *The Narrative Reader* (London: Routledge, 2000), p. 109. Barthes is also quoted in Young and Saver, "Neurology of Narrative."

5 Clifford Geertz, *The Interpretation of Cultures: Selected Essays* (New York: Basic Books, 1973), pp. 28–29, 5.

6 Lois Bloom, *Language Development from Two to Three* (Cambridge, UK: Cambridge University Press, 1993), p. 333.

7 Georg Wilhelm Friedrich Hegel, *Philosophy of History*, trans. John Sibree (New York: American Home Library, 1902), pp. 63–64, 164.

8 David Carr, "Narrative and the Real World: An Argument for Continuity," in Lewis P. Hinchman, ed., *Memory, Identity, Community: The Idea of Narrative in the Human Sciences* (SUNY Series in the Philosophy of the Social Sciences) (Albany, NY: SUNY Press, 1997), pp. 7–25.

9 François Dosse, *New History in France: The Triumph of the Annales*, trans. Peter V. Conroy Jr. (Champaign: University of Illinois Press, 1994), quote from p. 158.

10 Lawrence Stone linked the revival of narrative that he saw taking place at the end of the 1970s to "the end of the attempt to produce a coherent scientific explanation of change in the past," but he too missed the necessary connection between narrative and causal explanation. Lawrence Stone, "The Revival of Narrative: Reflections on a New Old History," *Past and Present* 85 (November, 1979): 3–24, quote from p. 19; Arthur C. Graesser, Murray Singer, and Tom Trabasso, "Constructing Inferences during Narrative Text Comprehension," *Psychological Review* 101 (1994): 371–395; Paul Ricoeur, *Time and Narrative*, vol. 1, trans. David Pellauer (Chicago: University of Chicago Press, 1990), fn. 23 on p. 254. David Carr, cited in an earlier note, is influenced by Ricoeur's views. Both are writing in the phenomenological tradition.

11 See the forum on "Progress in History?," in *Historically Speaking: The Bulletin of the Historical Society* (May/June, 2006).

12 Jan de Vries, "The Limits of Globalization in the Early Modern World," *Economic History Review* 63, no. 3 (2010): 710–733.

13 Anne Charlton, "Medicinal Uses of Tobacco in History," *Journal of the Royal Society of Medicine* 97, no. 6 (June 2004): 292–296.

14 Erika Monahan, "Locating Rhubarb: Early Modernity's Relevant Obscurity," in Paula Findlen, ed., *Early Modern Things: Objects and Their Histories, 1500–1800* (London: Routledge, 2012), pp. 227–251.

15 See, in particular, Ulinka Rublack and Pamela Selwyn, trans.,

"Fluxes: The Early Modern Body and the Emotions," *History Workshop Journal* 53 (April 1, 2002): 1–16.

16   In addition to ibid., see Mary Lindemann, *Medicine and Society in Early Modern Europe* (Cambridge, UK: Cambridge University Press, 2010).

17   The problem of evidence for this kind of analysis has been very usefully discussed in Jeremy Trevelyan Burman, "History from Within? Contextualizing the New Neurohistory and Seeking Its Methods," *History of Psychology* 15, no. 1 (2012): 84–99. It should be clear from Burman and from what I argue here how much I have been stimulated by Daniel Smail's work, *On Deep History and the Brain* (Berkeley: University of California Press, 2008).

18   Marie de Rabutin-Chantal, marquise de Sévigné, *Correspondance*, vol. 2: *1675–1680*, ed. Roger Duchêne (Paris: Gallimard, 1974), p. 133; Louis-Sébastien Mercier, *Panorama of Paris: Selections from Le Tableau de Paris*, ed. Jeremy D. Popkin (University Park, PA: Penn State Press, 1999), p. 97; Colin B. Bailey et al., *The Age of Watteau, Chardin, and Fragonard: Masterpieces of French Genre Painting* (New Haven, CT: Yale University Press, 2003).

19   Jason Hughes, *Learning to Smoke: Tobacco Use in the West* (Chicago: University of Chicago Press, 2003), pp. 73–77.

20   G. J. Barker-Benfield, *The Culture of Sensibility: Sex and Society in Eighteenth-Century Britain* (Chicago: University of Chicago Press, 1996), esp. p. 159.

21   Henry Morley, ed., *The Spectator, in Three Volumes*, vol. 1 (London: George Routledge, 1891), no. 10, March 12, 1711, at http://www.gutenberg.org/files/12030/12030-h/12030-h/SV1/Spectator1.html#section10 (consulted September 24, 2013).

22   Paul A. Shackel, *Personal Discipline and Material Culture: An Archaeology of Annapolis, Maryland, 1695–1870* (Knoxville: University of Tennessee Press, 1993).

23   For Mercier, see *Panorama of Paris*, p. 97. Beatrice Hohenegger, *Liquid Jade: The Story of Tea from East to West* (New York: Macmillan, 2006).

24   Sévigné, *Correspondance*, vol. 2: *1675–1680* (1974), p. 729; *Correspondance*, vol. 3: *1680–1696* (Paris: Gallimard, 1978), p. 1036.

25   Steve Pincus, " 'Coffee Politicians Does Create': Coffeehouses and Restoration Political Culture," *Journal of Modern History* 67, no. 4 (December 1, 1995): 807–834.

26   W. Scott Haine, *The World of the Paris Café: Sociability among the French Working Class, 1789–1914* (Baltimore, MD: Johns Hopkins University Press, 1998), p. 7.

27   On coffee consumption, see E. M. Jacobs, *Merchant in Asia: The Trade of the Dutch East India Company during the Eighteenth Century* (Leiden: CNWS, 2006).

28   I have found particularly helpful Alfred Schutz, *The Phenomenology of the Social World*, trans. George Walsh and Frederick Lehnert (Evanston, IL: Northwestern University Press, 1967).

29   *Reflections on the Revolution in France: and on the proceedings in certain societies in London relative to that event. In a letter intended to have been sent to a gentleman in Paris. By the Right Honourable Edmund Burke* (first published 1790; London: J. Dodsley, 1793), p. 11.

30   Ibid., p. 106. For swinish multitude, see p. 117.

31   Letter of January 1800 quoted in Lynn Hunt and Margaret Jacob, "The Affective Revolution in 1790s Britain," *Eighteenth-Century Studies* 34, no. 4 (Summer, 2001): 491–521, p. 497.

32   Ibid.

33   Quoted in ibid., p. 498.

34   Janet Afary and Kevin B. Anderson, *Foucault and the Iranian Revolution: Gender and the Seductions of Islamism* (Chicago: University of Chicago Press, 2010), p. 23.

35   Pieter Cornelis Spierenburg, *The Prison Experience: Disciplinary Institutions and Their Inmates in Early Modern Europe* (New Brunswick, NJ: Rutgers University Press, 1991).

36   See the useful overview in Norval Morris and David J. Rothman, eds., *The Oxford History of the Prison: The Practice of Punishment in Western Society* (Oxford, UK: Oxford University Press, 1995).

37   Hans Joas, *The Sacredness of the Person: A New Genealogy of Human*

Rights, trans. Alex Skinner (Washington, DC: Georgetown University Press, 2013). I have developed a parallel argument in Lynn Hunt, *Inventing Human Rights* (New York: W. W. Norton, 2007).

38   Wim Weymans, "Revising Foucault's Model of Modernity and Exclusion: Gauchet and Swain on Madness and Democracy," *Thesis Eleven* 98 (August, 2009): 33–51.

39   It is impossible to list all the works relevant to this point, but an important point of departure is Wolfgang Schivelbusch, *Tastes of Paradise: A Social History of Spices, Stimulants, and Intoxicants* (New York: Vintage Books, 1993).

40   *The Women's Petition Against Coffee . . . By a Well-Willer* (London, 1674).

INDEX